Trained for Abuse

Alisa Dawn Wilson

Copyright Registration Number: Insert Copyright Number

ISBN: 978-1-966901-72-3 (Ebook)

ISBN: 978-1-966901-91-4 (Paperback)

ISBN: 978-1-966901-90-7 (Hardback)

Disclaimer

This memoir contains sensitive content, including detailed accounts of child abuse, sexual assault, domestic violence, substance use, and emotional trauma. Some material may be emotionally difficult to read. Please prioritize your well-being and consider seeking support if needed as you move through the story.

Dedication

I dedicate this book to my children:

Jason James, Adriana Isabella, and Avery Jade.

Being your mother is my greatest strength. I will never stop fighting to give you the life you deserve.

Acknowledgments

First and foremost, I would like to acknowledge God. Thank You for giving me a soft and forgiving heart. For making me unbreakable. For giving me the strength to push through all of my abuse and rise above it.

I would also like to acknowledge the angels who showed up on my behalf. A simple thank you could never be enough. You are part of my success. Your kind words, thoughts, and actions helped me survive.

Lastly, I want to acknowledge anyone and everyone who has suffered abuse at the hands of those who claimed to love them. You are not alone. You are not your trauma. And you matter. Tell your story. You never know who needs your voice. Be the change, and rise above.

About the Author

Contents

Chapter 1
Conditioning

Some of my earliest memories are of trauma and abuse. I was born into a unit of five siblings: three older and one younger. My brother Donald being the oldest: Marie, Diane, myself, and May. Donald was born in '72, Marie in '75, Diane in '82, me in '85, and May in '87. I was born in Washington State, but I spent most of my life in NJ.

I remember being thrown into the back of a station wagon, being forced to leave my home, my father, and my best friend (Brandy, a dog) at the age of 3 to travel to NJ. My mother, Joyce, always said it was because my father, Rick, had a gambling problem, and she warned him to stop or she was going to leave. He didn't listen, so she left.

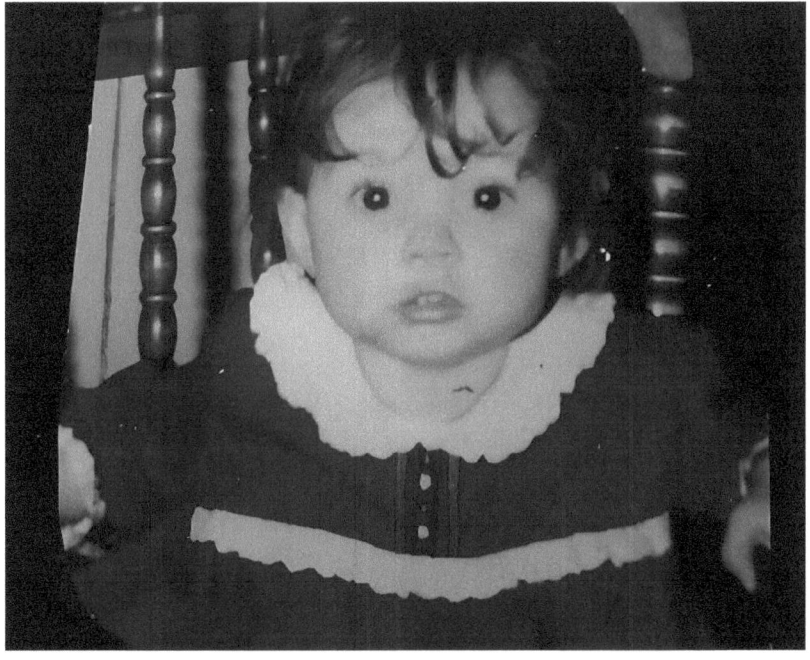

Me as a baby.

Left to right (back row): Possibly my grandma, my brother Donald with my sister Diane on his shoulders, and my grandpa John. Front row: an unknown person holding me (in red), my sister Marie, and another unknown person with a dog. Photo taken in Washington.

My mother Joyce, my brother Donald, and half of my sister Marie, back when we were all still together.

I recently found out from my half-sister Nancy it was more related to the neglect and abuse of me, Diane, and May. My father wanted custody of us and my mother wasn't having it, so she packed us up and took off. Ages 0–3 I would consider the best years of my life because I truly imagined a loving family/home/life. It was a feeling I would spend a lifetime chasing without success.

My arrival to NJ, to my recollection, wasn't horrible. I remember briefly living in Edgewater with my sister Marie's family, who I refer to as my aunt and uncle. Harold Donnie Wilbur (my sister Marie's dad), Judy Wilbur (my sister's aunt), Lauren Garris (my sister's cousin), and my grandma Helen Wilbur ♡, my absolute most favorite person who loved me like her own.

I don't remember my mother staying with us during that time. I remember it being just me, Diane, and May. We were in Edgewater a few months before moving to Marshall Ave in Little Ferry.

After a few months in our new apartment is when shit started getting serious. My sister Marie suffers from dissociative identity disorder, also known as multiple personalities. Her personalities were not fond of me. Their anger was aimed at just me. No one else.

My earliest memory of my sister Marie is of her trying to kill me. I was 4. Left alone with her, Diane, and May while my mother was working for a cab company. Marie threw me off the top bunk bed and I started crying. This made her/them angry. She stripped me naked and threw me into a tub of ice water, opened the window in the bathroom, and collected snow from outside to pile on top of me.

I don't remember how long I was there for, but I remember not being able to stop shaking or crying. I remember begging her to let me out and she just kept screaming for me to die. A small 6-year-old girl from the apartment building heard my cries and helped me sneak out of a small window and climb down a ladder. She hid me in her apartment until the cops came. Her name was Rayna. (Angel #1 sent by GOD.)

Her mother passed from AIDS shortly after this moment and I never heard from her again.

I can only assume that my sister Marie was placed in a facility after this, but I honestly don't know. I just remember her not living with us after that. We moved to Union Avenue (Little Ferry) after this. My mother Joyce met a man named Simon and he moved in. She started using crack.

We were poor. When I say poor… I mean the absolute worst. Clothes that didn't fit… shoes that didn't fit… no food… sometimes weeks without electricity. I remember using paper food stamps at the convenience store to purchase my mother's cigarettes. This was when you could bring a note and pick up groceries without an adult. Although I don't remember her ever buying much food with them.

My mother Joyce never worked after this. She became evil. Truly evil. Everything that went wrong in her life was because she had me, Diane, and May. She beat us. She starved us. She would lock us out of the house for hours to fend for ourselves. I'm small, guys. Maybe 5–6 years old. Roaming the streets. With my 7–8-year-old sister and my 4–5-year-old sister. This would become a normal thing for us for the next few years.

Our house was a crack house. Filthy… dirty… random users… abuse. We were always told that what happens in our house stays in our house. If we were to raise any flags, we would be beat. We were beat regardless.

I remember telling my teacher that I didn't have dinner in 1st grade, and she called home concerned. My mother beat me so badly with a mirrored paddle I couldn't attend school for 3 days. That was the last time I told anyone anything.

Me and my siblings had different experiences. Diane became resentful… rebellious. May was Simon's favorite because she was the smallest, so she really had it easier than me and Diane, at least that's how it seemed to me, being a small child. I became a people pleaser.

I truly believed in my heart that my mother would love me if I was better. So... I became better.

I'm now in 1ˢᵗ grade. I am the helper. The cleaner. The fixer. If Joyce wouldn't clean, then I would. If Joyce wouldn't cook, then I would. May was my responsibility. This quest for perfection only made Joyce hate me more. The more attempts I made at making her happy, the more she beat me. There were no happy holidays or birthday celebrations. She only cared about getting high. 🐵

My brother Donald and his wife Laura briefly moved home after the birth of my nephew Nico. My brother was suffering from something mentally. I personally witnessed him place my baby nephew on some kind of satanic board, asking Satan to accept him as his sacrifice. This scared me so badly that I threatened to tell. So, he kicked me down a flight of stairs. His defense was "that I was levitating." (Drugs are bad, kids... mmmkay.) I broke my arm. But records state that I'm just a clumsy kid who liked to climb trees.

My brother would move out shortly after this and I wouldn't see him again.

My attention turned to outside strangers for love and support. I knew that if I could not find help myself, I would never survive. So, I found it. Ms. Balone, an 80-year-old woman who lived across the street. She liked to garden. She had cookies. 🍪 I was a starving kid, so we started an exchange program for them. Garden help for food. ♡ 🙏 Thanks, God.

I also had Ms. Millie D., a 70-year-old cat lover who also had a love for snacks. Again, we began a similar exchange program... cat help (clean-up) for food. And I had school. Although the free three-tier PB & J was sufficient... it scars me to this day. 😬

I became the overachiever at school as well. Being smart, helpful, and loving makes people want to help. Right? Straight A's. Gifted and talented. Basketball. The longer I stayed away from home, the safer I was.

During the course of 1ˢᵗ–3ʳᵈ grade, I was molested seven times by three people: a local police officer who had a thing for obscene troll cards that I remember him forcing me to hang on the Dunkin' Donuts wall on Route 46 by the split, a clergyman from the local church on Marshall Ave (which I attended frequently with a sweet girl named Corrina, whose family treated me well), and a fellow user/close friend of my mother who would frequently sneak into my room while visiting. This is where I learned disconnect. 🙏

3ʳᵈ grade, I committed my first sin. 😌 There was a good friend of mine named Janet who had this special doll. It talked and moved. And I never had much unless it came used. I wanted it so badly. So, I took it. I brought it home and quickly hid/played with it in my closet. A few hours passed and I'm confident that I am in the clear. But let me tell you... Mrs. Marks was not having it. And sure as shit, this woman pulled up to my house causing such a scene, I thought for sure I would be killed that night.

Of course, I returned it. Cried. Apologized. She left after banishing me from ever returning. That night I had to pick my switch for my beating. Puts 40 lashes into a new perspective. I didn't pick a strong enough branch because I remember my mother switching to the belt. As long as my clothes hid the marks, she didn't care.

Now, as a child, you would assume that the anger behind this beating would stem from me stealing? 😵 It was, in fact, because she arrived at our house while my mother was getting high and she had to pretend to not be. So, this is where my need for timing control arrives. Problem was, she was always high. This lesson taught me that every choice has a consequence, and stealing was not for me.

I would love to say that the beating I endured was enough to stray me from sin. However, that was not the case.

A few months after this incident, I was at the Paramus Park Mall with a "new" friend. Sadly, I only remember her last name, which was

Sutherland. We were the same age, 3rd grade, so maybe 9. She was well off. Her family had money. Love. Happiness. My friend was entitled. Very demanding and assertive with her mother and typically got her way. We were dropped off to shop. Her mother gave her money to buy whatever she wanted.

She liked the high of stealing and did it frequently. I was unaware of this until the moment presented. We were in Claire's, and she was taking tons of things and stuffing them wherever she could. She encouraged me to do the same. Now me... remembering that last beating, strongly declined. She put stuff in my bag anyway. For herself. Because now… she had no more space.

We get caught. Of course. This incident included a beating and 3 months of community service. Lesson learned = sometimes you are guilty because of the company that you keep. Also known as guilty by association. Taught me to watch the company that I keep.

So, let's do a rundown of what I have learned, years 0–10.

Sometimes the people you love do not love you back, regardless of how much you love them. Words hurt. Is it kind? Necessary? True? ...Yes? ...Proceed. No? ...Shut up.

A house is not a home.
My body is just a vessel.
If you tell, you will suffer.
If you complain, you will suffer.
Be helpful and not a handful.
People in power use their power for control.
Strangers will help you faster than your loved ones.
Make sure you got yourself.
Just because they are expected to help does not mean they will.
Blend in, keep quiet, stay humble.

The more darkness that I lived through only filled me with more light, love, compassion, empathy. I felt sorry for these people. In my little world, they were just as broken as me. Although I was the one being hurt, I never saw myself as a victim. I knew that I had GOD. I knew He would always send me help. Retaliation and self-pity would only lead to a darkened heart.

And the most important: what happened to me had nothing to do with me. That's on them. I'm responsible for me.

Although I was able to process my reality early, it was lonely. Dark. I had a lot of questions that no one wanted to give me answers to. There weren't many "safe" places for me to go. Most of the people who were around me during this time were liars. Abusers. Manipulators. Narcissists. People who tried to convince me that I should be okay with what I was enduring. The evil deeds that were unfolding before my eyes. And to shut up about it.

These things never sat right with me in my soul. Especially when religion was often used as a cover for the situations that hurt me the most.

Kids were mean to me. Ruthlessly brutal. I was the stinky kid. The poor kid. The dirty kid. (And I was.) By no fault of my own.

I did manage to get a couple of great friends during 3rd–6th grade. Shane (who became my daughter's father), Jerry (another abused child who personally witnessed abuse and endured many outside adventures with me and protected me). Although we are no longer in communication, I am grateful and thankful for who you were to me during this difficult time. 🙏♡

And Shayla, my best friend who was deaf. Love and gratitude to Sherry (Shayla's mom) and her whole family, really. They helped care for me and provide for me when they never had to. 🙏♡ Forever grateful. I love you all.

Shannon (Shane's mother), although you hated me during these years because your son stole your engagement ring and gave it to me 😬, you led me to angel #2 sent from GOD just for me: Jack Sparks. 🙏♡

8

He will have a big chunk of my future years. Still grateful for you, ma. You loved me when you didn't have to. I love you. Thank you.

Now to tell you about Jack. He was a dirty ol' country man with a southern accent. His favorite terms were "how come" and "hey pretty lady." Jack had a house on Merhoff Road next to the skate park. Jack basically moved me into his home. Unofficially, of course. But he basically gave me my own safe place. He paid for my meals, my clothes. He gave me a job with him delivering shoes, so I could provide for myself. ♡ 🙏

Jack Sparks – my personal angel ♡

He would take me to fun places to just be a kid… all children, really. And he would always pay for us all. A very giving and caring man. I owe him everything and always showed my love and gratitude. I will forever miss him. He will reappear in a later entry, and often. He was truly GOD's personal angel in my life.

There was also another man I need to mention here, a very special teacher who helped me from 4th to 6th grade whenever he could: Mr. Harry Lagerman. This man will be the reason I'm finally removed from my home. He listened. He helped. 🙏♡ Not sure if he has passed, but I will always be grateful for the fight you fought on my behalf. You became a role model for me.

3rd–6th grade wasn't bad apart from a few incidents I'll dive into later. Although my home atmosphere didn't change, I had a support system at this point. I spent a lot of my free time working with Jack and spending time outside with my friends.

Once I reached 6th grade, I was enrolled into the Big Sister/Big Brother program through DYFS. Now let's not forget that DYFS had been involved since the initial incident with my sister Marie. They came to my home frequently, were aware of the conditions of my home, and the chronic drug problem that Joyce had. This program basically took underprivileged children and linked them with adult volunteers to allow the children to be children. We would go to fun places and events, completely paid for by the program.

This is where I would meet two very important people in my life: Anna "Nappy" Hudson (another child within the program who will become my best friend) and Dana Shulman, the woman who was my Big Sister volunteer but became my foster mother.

Now to dive into those incidents, I need to backtrack and fill in some blanks.

Simon, my mother's boyfriend? 😬... dealer, was a heavy-set Dominican man with a heavy accent. He spoke Spanish. He pretty much supplied an allotment to my mother of crack daily. Now when I say dealer, I want you to think of the dealers you see in the movies. To the naked eye, you would not even consider him to think about drugs, never mind sell them, but he did. By the brick.

I remember him having a safe in their bedroom and it would be filled with drugs. Simon did not use drugs. Simon was a top player. He knew exactly what he had to do to keep my mother where she was.

Now when I say we didn't have any money, we didn't. But he did. Thousands. Everything was kept inside his safe in their bedroom. Whenever my mother could, she would try and break into it. For the drugs of course... not the money. And I remember this one time he found out that she opened it and he went after her with a knife.

I'm maybe 12 now, and naturally, I try to intervene. I managed to get between them before he got her, but it left me with a shallow scar across my chest.

I was sent to stay with my Aunt Judy in Florida after this incident. This is where I will tell my first lie. Well obviously, I had been lying my whole life about what was going on at home, but I never saw it as lies because it was literally what kept me safe.

My Aunt Judy and Uncle Donnie frequently came to my rescue when shit got serious at home. I had been with my aunt for a few weeks at this point in Satellite Beach, FL, and she had let me borrow one of her necklaces. I broke it. Accidentally, of course.

I was so afraid for my safety that I hid it. Now my Aunt Judy never hit me. She was one of the few people in my life who truly cared for me. But in my head... I was done for. So I hid it.

This necklace must have meant something to her because she confronted me about where it was since I hadn't been wearing it. Naturally, I tried to lie and say it was lost. She must have been psychic because she was not having it. She screamed and yelled and made threats until I finally told her the truth.

I returned it to her broken, and I was hysterical. She bought me a plane ticket for the first flight home. That was the last time I would see or speak with my Aunt Judy.

This is when I learned that honesty was important. If I am safe, I should tell the truth. Even if it hurts.

Once I arrived home, everything was back to normal. Just another day in paradise, so they say.

I'm still spending as much time as possible away from the house. I'm involved in sports. I have my own income. I have my own room at Jack's for safety. I have great friends, and they had pretty decent families who always provided for me. So naturally, I'm feeling confident that things are looking up.

We're now looking at heading into 7th grade. I have to say here and now that I can't account for anything anyone else went through at this time, or anytime during this story. These are *my* personal experiences. How *I* felt. What *I* experienced. I'm not trying to make anyone feel guilty or feel sorry for me. I promise you that I am okay. I have always been okay. And that is the main point.

I'm trying to be honest. The truth, the whole truth, and nothing but. From my account. Why I am the person that I am. Why my heart is the way that it is. I am truly hoping that this helps others on many levels. I will do my best to tell my story without hurting anyone. ♡🙏

Ok, do you remember a few posts back when I mentioned that my baby sister was my responsibility? Ok. Well, I had not been doing my job very well. I'm young. She's young. I have friends, she has friends. We are hanging out on opposite sides of town. I'm at the Redneck Ave Park, playing with the cat lady's cats. May is at the tire park by the circle, maybe the distance of about two miles. Both of us on bikes.

She's headed toward us to see the cats (frequent activity for us and our friends). On her way, she is hit by a car. It's serious. She's taken immediately to the hospital.

Now, we are talking about the '90s here. There were no cell phones. We knew where people were by looking for their bikes. Payphones were still around and used often. I have no idea where my sister is. All I know is that she didn't show up at the park. So… I head home to see if she's there.

Now my sister Diane did not live at home during this time. Like I had previously mentioned, we all had different experiences. Diane had run away. Not sure of the specific details, but I know it was with a boyfriend. She had been gone a few months at this point.

My mother is not at the house. Simon was at the house.

Now Simon also beat me. As often as my mother beat me, he beat me. And like I said, May was Simon's favorite.

Now for visual purposes, our house on Union Ave had one main door. Two doors inside. Bottom and top floor apartments. We had the 2nd and 3rd floor, so door… door… steps… top of steps, to the right, bathroom and kitchen. To the left, living room, sunroom, stairs to two bedrooms.

The second my foot touched that top step, I took a belt to the face. Simon is livid. Cursing. Mostly in Spanish. Screaming that May was in the hospital, while beating me at the landing with a belt.

Now, I'm being whipped, people. I mean absolutely beaten. Yet instead of fleeing, I'm here asking specifics. I have one arm above my head, fighting the belt from my face, and I finally get the details, then I'm out.

This is the last time I'll step foot into my house.

I hop on my bike and book it back to Jack's. I'm a mess. Now anyone who knows me knows that you can't understand a damn thing I say when I am truly upset. Jack can't stand to see me upset, so now he's furious. I finally calm down and tell him what happened.

Now Jack wasn't fond of my mother for obvious reasons, but he played a good role for my benefit. He drove down to the hospital to see what was going on.

Now I'm safe. I'm in my room at Jack's, with my pet cat Tigger (Jack got just for me), and we are good. Although I wanted to go, I could not go for many reasons. Mainly due to the belt mark across the face, but also for my safety. Jack frequently told my mother that he hadn't seen me.

Jack finally returns and tells me that my sister has a broken leg. Concussion. Things are bad. DYFS is at the hospital. May would be admitted for a few weeks. So naturally, Jack told everyone that he hadn't seen me. ♡ 🙏 Truly my angel.

So now he's trying to come up with a plan for me.

I sneak out. My old teacher, Mr. Lagerman, lived about four blocks away from Jack. Mr. Lagerman knew I was abused but never forced me into any specific details. Was just very generous and patient and understanding. And he would always tell me, "Lisa… if you need my help, you say the word."

He was the aftercare program director at the elementary school. I frequented this program daily for food. Even though I did not pay. He always gave me food. 🙏 ♡

I rang his bell. He comes to the door. Sees me. Sees my face. And said, "Lisa, no matter what you say at this point, I have to call."

I said, "I'm ready, Mr. Lagerman. I just can't go home."

So he calls DYFS. Explains the situation. Explains that I want to stay at Jack's. Obviously, this can't happen. Jack was a middle-aged single man. Divorced. No females in the house. Besides me, and other local underprivileged children who would come for a safe place to be.

So the cops were aware of Jack and who he was to the local children.

Now I'm young still. I don't understand how any of this works. All I know is that I am safe at Jack's. And if I go home, I will die. And now my teacher, who has promised to help me, has just turned me into the fuzz.

As he is trying to explain why I have to go back home first, cops turn the block, and I'm out.

He's screaming after me to come back, but I wasn't having it. I sneak back into the park behind Jack's house to watch the show.

Obviously, I could not return to Jack's because the cops were there for me. So I'm just stuffed in some bushes, watching from a distance. After about an hour, they finally leave.

Now I'm still scared. I don't know if I should stay where I am or if I should go find out what the verdict is.

Naturally, I stay 🛴 safety first, people 🛴 safety first.

After about three hours, I finally build up enough courage to head back to Jack's. So, I cross the parking lot and head in. He's calm. Worried. Makes sure I'm good and sits me down. Basically explains to me that I cannot stay there because there was not a female guardian. My sister has been removed from my mother's care and will not be returning home. Neither will I.

I'm hysterical. He calms me down and explains to me that my mother has called my Aunt Brenda to come and take temporary custody of me, and she's catching the first flight. Now legally he cannot let me stay. But he did. 🙏♡

My Aunt Brenda was my mother's sister. I never met her. Never knew her. Never heard of her. On the rare occasion I was allowed inside our home, there was never any discussion about the family. Ever. Everything was private. I do not want to go with her. But I do not want to go somewhere else. So, I decide to wait it out.

She arrives, and Jack is approved for me to stay in his house. Legally now. But temporary, as long as my aunt is in the home. Neither me nor Jack know this woman, and now my life is in her hands.

At this point, I have been in contact with my volunteer big sister, Dana Shulman. I tell her what I know and what is going on, and she asks me if I want her to see if they would allow me to stay with her.

I said yes please 😓 🫨 🙏 🕯️

DYFS arranges a meeting with me and my sister Marie during this week. I haven't seen or spoken with her since I was four and she tried to kill me. Me, my caseworker, Marie, and her caseworker all meet at the pizza place on the corner of Merhoff Rd for lunch and visitation.

We all sit down for pizza. Everything is going well. Marie's caseworker leaves the table to grab our pizza, and Marie lunges at me out of nowhere. Once again screaming threats of death and harm. She is restrained in front of me. This will be the last time I ever see my sister Marie. I'm pretty sure she was placed in Greystone after this, but I can't be positive. No one told me much.

I'll return to Jack's.

So me and Jack are getting to know my Aunt Brenda. She seems ok. A little eccentric. Bouncy. She's really diving deep, pushing the good life with her back in Washington. Tells me about my cousins. My flags are up.

She's there about a week at this point, and it's a strong no for me. Something is up. I don't know much, but I know when I am being played. And she was playing.

I'm still waiting for news. News from Dana. News from DYFS. News from my sister. And I got nothing. I am panicking at this point, and my head is in a million places. Every ounce of me just wanted to run away. Guaranteed safety. But I stuck it out. Headed to school.

This will be the last time I am in Jack's house.

I'm in 7th grade. I haven't spoken to Mr. Lagerman since I arrived at his door over a week prior and then took off. He's a 6th grade teacher. He sees me, immediately apologizes for my experience, and asks for an update. I fill him in on what I know. He apologizes again for my suffering and invites me to his room for pizza at lunch. Then I head to class.

Lunch arrives and I head down to Mr. Lagerman's, and all of my friends are there. Plenty of pizza. And those disposable cameras. He said they were to capture the moment, a comment that won't click inside my head for about an hour's time. We had the best lunch. ♡ 🙏

Mr. Harry Lagerman – My Last Day in Little Ferry

These will be the last moments I spend in Little Ferry.

2-9-1999 — "D" Day.

I have just enjoyed the most delicious pizza lunch/party. Me and my friends are enjoying some outdoor recess when I am suddenly called inside. I head into the office and there's DYFS.

17

Me in 7ᵗʰ Grade

Good ol' Wendy Mascotti Come to place me as a ward of the state. Number 647-483-264 😵 🤢 🤖 maybe.

Heeerreeee she comes to save the day 🦸 🦸

I truly can't say anything bad about her. She was new to our caseload, so she wasn't really responsible for the obvious neglect of our system. She basically said we were headed out. And to say my goodbyes. So, I did.

And I got in her car. And I remember there being a small suitcase next to me in that car that didn't belong to me but now belonged to me. And we left. Me and my cameras. And a new bag. Headed who knows. With a lady I barely know. Taken away from everything I have ever known.

In an instant. To arrive at my new life.

I would refer to these previous years as my "conditioning" period. Because at this point, I've already survived everything. I am confident in who I am. And I know what I have endured. And most importantly… I know that I have GOD. 🙏

Now before I start my next "chapter," I want to pause and give you more of a visual of the previous years.

So, our house on Union Ave was a dump. The typical atmosphere was filthy, and it had a very strong smell of pet urine/feces. We had roaches. We had mice. We rarely had electricity, so my mother barely cooked. And when she did, her go-to meal was chicken on the bone and rice with beans. A meal I would never be able to consume after these years.

Our house was only clean on the days I cleaned it, typically on the days DYFS would visit. Because like I had previously stated, I was not welcome in our home during daylight hours. The only time my mother was a mother was during these times. We would clean the house, put on our cleanest clothes, and pretend to be a happy family.

We did not have a washing machine. We would take our laundry once a month to the Laundromat. In between washes, you would find massive amounts of dirty clothes mixed with fecal matter, trash, and roaches throughout our home.

Now, being an abused child, I had a very special love for animals. But… my mother's animals were sent straight from hell. She had a Pekinese that bit, didn't listen, and consistently defecated throughout the house. And she also had a Siamese cat who would randomly attack me and my sisters without cause.

I remember having an ear infection in 5th grade. It was so bad. I cried and cried, and my mother would not listen. This went on for about two weeks. I couldn't deal with the pain anymore, so I took myself down to the nurse. Explained to her that I couldn't get my mom to listen, so she takes a look. Sure as shit, I had a dead roach stuck inside my ear. She was finally able to pull it out, and bam. Instant relief.

This specific incident will cause me to have severe PTSD with ALL insects/rodents. I love ya… but stay away. 🤢 🙏

The nurse called home to tell my mother what she found. I walked into a beating that afternoon. People ask me... why didn't you say anything? Why weren't you more vocal about what you were dealing with?

Because I learned in first grade, that you have to save yourself. No one is coming. Everyone has a sad story, and I would never be a "woe is me" child. I took every lash as a battle scar. Taught myself to love it. Be grateful for it. Thank you, it felt nice. 🙏

I did not have a lot of role models. I had a lot of people I didn't want to end up like. I was a kid. An unwanted, unloved, neglected child. And the people who were supposed to be protecting me became the people I needed protection from.

My sister Diane was vocal. Very vocal. Hence the rebellion. No one listened. No one cared. I saw her rebellion as a marker for why not to tell. I'm sure she endured her own hidden suffering during this time. Unspoken. She definitely was the epitome of a child with home problems.

My mother painted her to be the cause of our home problems. She wasn't. She was innocent. She was a child. Whatever behaviors she displayed during this period of our lives were due to my mother's abuse. This period will change my sister's heart forever. So please take this entry and remember it for the future posts.

Turns out my Aunt Brenda also had a drug problem. Speed. She obviously was denied custody of me. This is a common trait on my mother's side. Her and her siblings were all addicted to something, with their children being in similar situations as me and my siblings.

I was happy I didn't have to go with her. She resembled my mother too much. Her promise to "help" threw up all my flags. Because like I said, something was up. From the second I met her, I knew. And if she truly did care for me... where had she been? Where had any of my "family" members been?

I remember only my Grandpa John, who wasn't even my mother's true father. He's the only one who ever called. Ever reached out. And he lived far, Washington State. No one ever visited besides my Uncle Donnie and Aunt Judy. Everyone else who came in our home was a fellow user/buyer.

Joyce wasn't shy about her drug problem with me or my sisters. She frequently would light up right in front of us. I'm pretty sure I had seen enough "mixing" before 2nd grade that I could have made the rocks myself. Little coke… baking soda… water… mix it up… light her till she balls 😷🎈 sad but I have to laugh.

This is where I develop my dark humor, people. These are those moments.

We often made drug runs over the bridge. Me and my sisters dreaded these moments. She would typically pick one of us to ride with her as cover. She would chain smoke cigarettes with the windows up both ways and then leave us in the car alone while she went inside.

One specific time, I remember me and both of my sisters being left for hours in Dyckman Park, right off the Henry Hudson. Must have been after midnight when we left. This is one of the rare times Simon came for the pickup. We were never invited in. And always left alone.

Although I can continue, these moments are the moments that truly built my core.

I did have good moments as well. And I truly am grateful for both sides. The good with the bad. They both made me. The lessons and choices I made during this time taught me many things.

I'm sorry I couldn't save us 😔 that no one could. It took me a very long time to accept that it wasn't my responsibility. And that every single person who caused me harm during these moments were all suffering from their own demons.

But I'm so grateful that it never changed who I am. 🙏

Anyone who knew me during this time knows that my heart is still the same, if not bigger. My compassion and empathy are always present. And I always try to show up as my best self. Even when it's hard. Even when I don't want to. Because WE have to be the change.

Just because this is what you know doesn't mean you have to repeat the pattern.

Although I may have been a bummer lamb, I know my Father's voice 🙏 and these patterns… stopped with me.

Truth is… we are all a little messed up. Some of us are just more honest about it. 🐵

Chapter 2
Pending

So here I am, at my new life. Me, my cameras, and my brand-new suitcase which holds 🐵. Haven't peeked yet.

Honestly, my emotions were all over the place. I was sad, angry, scared, nervous, happy, excited. All at once. No one told me what was going on. This was a typical thing with the adults in my life.

I wasn't sure where I was, but it was a quiet street. A nice two-story house in Garfield. Very presentable. I'm trying my hardest not to cry, which is my typical response to most situations. I knew I needed to be strong. And at this point, all I'm thinking is whatever lies behind that front door had to be better than what I had already endured.

Wendy asks me if I'm ready. Of course I am not, but I exit the vehicle anyway. She grabs the suitcase and walks beside me to the door. We ring the bell, and we wait.

Me and Wendy

Behind the door is Bill (my foster dad). Now, I have met Bill a few times at this point while interacting with the Big Sister/Big Brother program. I had accompanied him and Dana a few times out to dinner. He was a quiet man. Didn't say much, but often made jokes and had a way of making people truly feel welcomed.

I feel instant relief at this point. I know that I am at Dana's house. I know that I will be safe. I'm just unsure of the specifics.

We head upstairs. Dana and Bill had a 3-bedroom apartment on the top floor. No kids. Just a cat named Tommy. They had a bedroom already prepared for me, showed me around the house, and then sat down to talk with Wendy. Not sure what was discussed at this point because I decided to stay in my new room. With my new suitcase. Cameras. And emotions.

I finally open my new suitcase to find a few new outfits, personal hygiene products, and a pair of sneakers which were larger than my actual size. This fact didn't bother me... I grew up wearing shoes typically 2–3 sizes smaller. Or whatever my mother was gifted. Until I started buying my own with Jack.

I stayed in that room until dinner. Not for any other reason than being unsure of how to be. We had pizza. Again. Then I headed to bed. I cried myself to sleep. Not really sure why. Probably just scared of what was to come looking back but 🤷. I'm a crier.

My new home was different. Managed properly. Clean. Stocked. There were rules. No more worrying about taking care of myself. Chores. Curfew. A total 180 from my old life.

I didn't care. I was happy to not be beaten.

The rest of 7th grade was rough. I tried to keep to myself. Stay low. Blend in. Keep my grades up. Dana and Bill worked full time, so I attended the Boys and Girls Club aftercare program. This is where I will meet my best friends: Anna "Nappy" Hudson (who I already knew), Michelle Wallace, Jessica and Jenny Brooks, Theresa Lawrence, and Melissa Sampson.

Truly grateful for these women right here. 🙏 You all helped me through a very difficult transition and never treated me like I was less than. Thank you. ♡

The summer before 8th grade is truly when we got close. To dive into this period, I need to dive into my relationship with Anna.

Nappy was a troubled girl. She had a rough life. Been through some horrible situations. Me and Nappy had an instant connection. We had met before I was removed, at a BS/BB function. She basically told me her life story within the first few minutes of meeting.

Nappy had the need for excitement. She typically acted out. Got in trouble. And often made a scene. It was always a fun time when she was around. She reminded me a lot of my sister Diane, but with more of a feisty spirit.

She was my absolute best friend.

Me and Nappy – Meeting at a Big Brothers/Big Sisters Function

Nappy, being the bright ball of light that she was, had a lot of friends. She was always on the move. She didn't take correction well and did not respect authority. She knew EVERY single secret from my life and never judged me. Never exposed me. Never betrayed me. Her friends became my friends.

We would often hang out at Danerts Lake Park or behind the school.

Nappy had some addictions. She liked to party. She really was down for trying anything. This part of Nappy scared me. I was the opposite. Her confidence in her safety was admiring but often got us into trouble.

Her friends kept her grounded. Nappy had a thing for the boys, so she would often drag us to house parties of older guys. Looking back, I think it was more for the free "fun." Her way of looking at life was "fuck it."

She often spoke about being dead inside, but if you knew Anna, her spirit told a different story. She was a fighter. A warrior.

I will learn two very important lessons during this point of my life.

I'm now entering 8th grade. Summer has ended, and I have accepted my new identity. I have great friends. I have a safe home. I'm well liked. Things are looking good.

I was a very shy kid. And with just cause. Didn't want anyone else to hurt me or touch me. Really just tried to blend in. I grew up being observant. This taught me that most people weren't who they pretended to be. I had no interest in playing along and only connected with a select few.

Being friends with beautiful girls always had us in the spotlight. I clinged to my old patterns. Started hanging out with Shane from my past and his group of friends. They lived in Lodi, so right up the hill from our normal hangout spot.

Jack was still very present in my life. He often picked me up for meals out or for fun times. Shane was Jack's grandson, removed through marriage, but still spent a lot of time with him. Shane was safe. Shane knew my story.

His group of friends meshed well with my group of friends, and we created a bond. Anna began dating Shane's best friend George, and I began dating Shane.

The end of September that year, my foster brother Dennis arrived. In the middle of the night. With few supplies. He was six weeks old and was born addicted to drugs. He was a difficult baby. Cried often. Was always sick. I was happy to not be alone. We didn't have much of a relationship that first year because of his issues, but he would grow on me with time.

Back to my personal life, I have now developed my first toxic trait.

Nappy was the opposite of me. Very open to her sexuality. She often made choices that I was uncomfortable with. But with us dating as a pair, we used this to our advantage.

We would often switch boyfriends when we were unhappy with their behaviors. Typically referred to between us as *switching off*. Other friends would jump on this boat as well, but their stories didn't really impact me. In our eyes, it was fair game.

This game went back and forth a few months until it ended abruptly. We all had enough, so we moved on. Still friends, of course.

Now, of course I joined the basketball team while I was here. It was a safety net for me. This is where Anna will meet her next encounter. He was an older boy named *****, referred to as Alabama. I cannot state a name here because I do not recall his last name and have not been able to find anyone who does. If you were present during these times, you will know who I am referring to.

Alabama was a very charismatic older boy. Another beacon of light, per se. He had just recently moved from down south and had a heavy southern accent. I don't know what rules he had at home, but Nappy always said his mom was "fun" (red flag). Rarely home.

I did not feel safe here. Me and Nappy would often visit. Could have been for the weed, but 🤷. She cared enough about me to keep it to herself.

The typical atmosphere was drinking, cigarettes, weed, partying. Me and most of our friends would typically wait outside for her. The door was always revolving. Never knowing who would emerge. And Alabama was quite popular and typically hung out in a group. He was an attractive guy.

Of course, Nappy stopped by frequently. I couldn't piece it together, and we frequently fought over it. She would just always say, "Don't worry about it. I'm good." I honestly didn't care what she did. Nappy could do no wrong in my eyes with what she had already endured. Our connection was truly divine.

One night we arrived at Alabama's and she dipped on me. Took off to a bedroom out of sight and left me on the couch with a group of older boys. I'm uncomfortable. Alone. Just me, her, Alabama, and two other boys.

This will be the first time someone attempts to rape me.

I was offered some weed, cocaine, beer. Of course, I declined. Never had any interest in even trying anything besides cigarettes. This made them mad. Kept telling me that I thought I was better than them. ☐ (I was?)

I was lifted and thrown onto the bed. I remember kicking and screaming while they tried to remove my clothes, to no avail. Alabama (Angel #3) saved me that night. There were punches thrown, and the boys swore they were just playing. 🙏

Because of this incident, I will avoid house parties. This was lesson #1 during this point.

We are now in November. I am awoken by Bill. He tells me buns are in the oven.

Of course, I run for food 🏃 Guess what? No breakfast.

The buns Bill was referring to were not the kind I could enjoy.

Surprise 🎉 🐣 guess who's having triplets?

I honestly didn't care. Where was my breakfast? Please don't judge me 🤭 🙏 I was a hungry teenager who was woken with disappointment.

I went back to bed.

When I finally woke up and processed what was going on, I was panicked. All I could think was that within a few short months they were about to have their own *real* children. And me and Dennis would most likely be booted out. Well, definitely me… possibly the baby.

I want to say that it was my friend Theresa Lawrence I cried it out with, but honestly, I cannot remember. Just remember being an emotional mess.

I rarely had sleepovers, unless they were at my house. Me and my friends were often on the move. This point of my life is when I felt the safest. ♡ I am so grateful for all the people I had in my life during this time. If I did not mention your name, I still love you and you are still important to me. These are just very specific moments that shaped my core. That's why there are some gaps. Maybe one day I'll do a tell-all 🤭 🙏

Guess who's got to move again? 🙎 Surprise 🎉 Dana and Bill fill me in on the plans for our big move come graduation. I'm angry but also relieved. I don't want to move. I finally belong. I have friends. People like me. I'm not referred to as the foster kid… or the dirty kid… or the poor kid. I'm just me.

In my head, I couldn't place a need for moving. We had three bedrooms. That was already one more than I grew up having, sharing with five people. How much more space can people need?

I know that either way I'm moving. If not with them, then with strangers. So, I had no choice but to just deal with it.

During this time, I'm still having supervised visits with my mother Joyce, who is still actively threatening me about being vocal and how she's doing everything in her power to get us back. (A lie I won't realize until I'm 38.) I rarely saw my biological siblings (May or Diane), maybe a total of three times after we were removed, until we became adults.

Left to right – Me, Diane, and May

May 11th, 2000, here come my siblings. ♡ Due to them being multiples, they came home at different times. Mary was the first to arrive and she was absolutely perfect. She's quiet. She's cute. I'm starting to think this will be ok. Other than the fact we still must move.

William will arrive soon after this, then Rose. That first month flew by, because I don't remember much other than them arriving home. The house was chaotic. Lots of cries. Lots of babies. Lots of stuff.

Helllooo graduation. My big day has arrived. After a quick ceremony, we go out for a meal, then head home. This is the moment I accept that the move is final. This night was my breaking moment.

Me and Bill – 8th Grade Graduation

Lesson #2: Never get too attached to anyone or anything.

I had created such a toxic attachment to my friends. They truly were my team, my pack 🐾 Because of this, I will avoid groups of females moving forward. Typically, only connecting with a select few.

We are now at the end of June. It's departure day. All my friends have come to see me off. We take tons of photos while I try and hold back my tears. This will be the last time I see Nappy until we are adults. Shortly after I leave, she will fall into a coma. 😔

And we pull off… once again. Off to my new life.

My rundown of lessons for this chapter was simple:

- The only time I will be safe is if I am by myself.
- Parties = problems.
- Strangers can help rebuild your broken parts better than the people you love.
- Belonging for a moment can create such a strong foundation. But at a moment's notice, it can all be ripped away.
- Still don't trust that I'm safe.
- Still don't trust that I won't have to return to Joyce.
- Definitely don't want to leave Jack. Or my friends.
- And now, I'm just a number in a horse corral.

Please understand that these were my feelings at this moment of my life. My experiences. I was not receiving therapy. No one talked about my past. No one talked about my present. And my future was always planned without my say.

I had Jack and Nappy.

And now… I have no one.

Once again.

Just two people that I am still trying to get to know, and four babies.

And a destination almost an hour away.

Chapter 3
Where the hell am I?

So, we take off. Just me and Bill in the moving truck, driving down Route 80. I remember a very deep sadness in my chest as my "new" old life got smaller in the side mirror. Sixteen short months of happiness. Acceptance. Safety.

The drive felt like it took forever. Bill was a man of few words. 🫤 Although he did speak, I don't recall his words. My mind was elsewhere. As an obedient child, I rarely ever got in trouble. I honestly was too scared. I mean, if my mother could beat me the way she used to, I could only imagine what someone else could do.

I was never physically harmed by Dana or Bill, but that didn't mean I didn't think they could. I'm still trying to figure them out. And I'm cautious. But every ounce of me wanted to run away back to Jack.

As we arrive in Hopatcong, reality kicks in. This is it. My new prison. Literally. No sidewalks. No streetlights. Barely any kids. All this town had to offer the kids was a teen club.

We pass a park in the center of town, and I see basketball courts. 😍 Now I'm feeling a little better. At least I have that. We pull up to the new house. Yyyaaayyy 🙄 lucky us. Here we are. A huge house in the middle of the woods. Probably so no one can hear the screams.

I don't remember unpacking. I just remember heading to the park with my ball. Now, coming from an urban area to the sticks... I stuck out. My typical attire during this time was shorts, a tank or undershirt, and work boots. 🥷 Gotta be ready for whatever calls. 🫤 I was comfortable. And I never really cared about what other people thought of me. I mean, I had been told who or what I was my whole life. But I wasn't any of those things. That was my circumstance. I couldn't change the outcome because it wasn't my battle. So, I just dismissed it, gave it to God, and departed. It truly is best.

When I finally made it to the park, my first thought was that I needed a bike. ⓐ Park was pretty dead. Two adults playing at the court and a few smaller kids in the playground. Great. They dragged me out to the dead zone.

I shoot around for a while. Park's still empty. I'm panicking. It's the beginning of the summer. I got no friends. Still working on trusting my parents. Now what?

So, I head into town. I have some cash Jack snuck me before I left. I was hungry, and there was a pizza place. So, I headed to Frank's Pizza. This was when it was next to the quick stop, by Walgreens, before the skatepark was installed.

I finally see some signs of life. ⓐ These kids were clearly older than me, but it was a start. I grab my slice and head out. Sit on the curb. Observe while I'm eating. I never took an interest in skateboarding, but it seemed to be the only sign of life here. Yikes. Where the hell am I?

I head home. I remember the next few weeks being hectic. Four babies, a new house, a new town. I'm depressed. And it must have shown because Bill suggested that I check out the teen club in town.

We are probably in July at this point. I had never been to a club. I truly just wanted some friends. I missed mine. And they were so far away now. So, I go.

Honestly, my first experience here wasn't so bad. Music was decent. There were kids. Not packed, but reasonably filled. I sit in the corner. My typical spot for visual purposes.

Now, I've probably been in town a total of five times before this night. There was only one person who spoke to me—an older boy people called Obie. He was genuine. Nice. Kind. A pure spirit. We had met about two weeks prior while on my way to Frank's. He was one of the skateboarders who hung out by quick stop.

He heads over to me. Starts small talk. Then out of nowhere, I'm bombarded with girls at the table. Now, I truly do not know anyone at this point, but I'm pretty sure that I have given you the idea of how this situation felt for me. Remember... I'm in a corner. There are maybe five to seven girls around me. They are all talking at once.

"Hey... you're the new girl, right?"

My response... "I guess." 😣 Like I said, not a very comfortable situation for me. I can tell that these are the popular girls. Many reasons, but the most obvious was the obnoxiousness. Over-talking. Gossiping.

Now, as a basketball player, I was quite familiar with these types of girls. Cheerleaders. 🙄 And let me just say that it wasn't a judgment. Just an observation of a child who was hyper-aware.

Within the first ten minutes of meeting these girls, they had already named half the school of people to avoid. I was never one for the gossip. There are many reasons why people talk. And frankly, none are my business. I really try to give everyone their fair shot at showing me who they are.

Now, I had picked up a bad habit back in Garfield. I was a smoker. It was my way of rebelling. I truly didn't enjoy it back then, but it helped me to not have to talk. 😣 🙄

In this club, no one harassed you over cigarettes. And many teens were smoking. So... I lit up... and the girls scattered. 😣 Probably best.

After visiting the club a few times, and the courts, I finally met someone I felt comfortable talking to. Of course, this turned out to be the absolute worst person I could have found. No name will be mentioned here, for many reasons. This boy was the town troublemaker, a bad boy with quite a reputation. I was new. I was clueless. But Bill knew. The first time he saw me with him, he told me he was trouble and warned me to stay away.

They said that about Nappy too, and she was an angel in my eyes. So, I dismissed it and started dating this boy. I liked to kiss (that's all that ever happened). He was a kisser. He was cute, had nice arm muscles, tattoos, and my parents didn't like him. These were all good things in my mind. 🐒 And I was looking for safety.

I dated this boy for three weeks. One day he invited me swimming. Now, I hadn't been swimming at the lake up to this point, but there was a local dock down from Modick Park that the kids would sneak to. I was excited to check it out and came prepared in my suit and usual attire.

I arrived at the park, and he told me we had to walk to his house so he could grab some shorts. So, we headed over. He lived close to the Quick Check, so it was a hike. It was hot. We finally got to his house, and he invited me in. Now, I knew better, but his older brother was home, so I went inside.

He led me straight to his room and told me to sit on the bed because he needed a few minutes. I did not sit. He left the room for a couple of minutes, and I just observed his space. It was messy. Not much color. 🐵

This was the second time someone would attempt to rape me. He tried to force himself on me. I pushed him away. He tried a second time, and my response was the same. He pushed me onto the bed and tried to climb on me. I was kicking and screaming. His brother came in, pulled him off of me, and asked what the hell he was doing. His response was that it was a joke.

He sure was.

His brother (Angel #4) told me I could go. So I left. We never officially broke up, but we never spoke again until I became an adult. And it wasn't in a hostile way. Just a "you never phased me" way. People know what they do. You'll never see me call it out unless we're together. You moved a certain way, and I moved aside. Be safe.

Now, because these are hometown details, I'm going to switch it up a little. Just because I own my behaviors doesn't mean I have the right to expose someone else. If you were present in my life during these next couple of years, you'll piece it together. If not 🙊 it's the lessons that matter. They made me.

I met my first female "friend" here. We'll call her Jessica. 🐥 Jessica was known around town as well. I wasn't sure of the specifics, but I didn't care. I needed some friends, and school was about to start. Jessica and I got close quickly. She smoked cigarettes and reminded me of Nappy. I was very wrong.

I would learn two more very important lessons during this year.

So, if you remember from earlier chapters, you know who Shane is. Shane had a cousin who also lived in Hopatcong. His name was Angelo. We called him Bubby. It was a nickname from his mother that stuck since he was a baby. Bubby lived by the Mud Hole. My house was over the River Styx bridge. Jessica's was in the middle. Shane would often visit Bubby.

Now, like I mentioned before, Shane was my safety net. And because of what I had just recently endured, I wasn't interested in seeing what else the town had to offer. So, I thought it best to try dating Shane again. Keep myself off the market. Safe.

That's really what it always came down to for me: safety. Shane loved me, but in a puppy dog kind of way. He also liked to play games. We'd been down this road quite a few times already. He was playing hard to get. 😵

Our relationship was mostly phone, AOL, and the occasional weekend that Bubby would let him come up.

One day, Jessica, Bubby, Shane, and I were all at Bubby's house. Jessica and I had known each other a few months by this point, and I thought we were pretty close. She knew my intentions with Shane. She knew why I didn't want to date anyone in town.

Needless to say, this would be the first time I was betrayed by a friend. I walked in on them making out. Her response was, "He prefers me." I was bitter. I responded with, "Enjoy him. He'll be back for me. He always is." And I went home.

This would help me choose my female friends differently.

To give you an idea of what my home atmosphere was like, it was nuts. The rules at home were simple: help clean, keep my grades up, help with the babies, and be home by dark. That was great in the summer, but please remember that we had six months when it got dark at 6 PM.

The first six months after the triplets were born were the worst. Basically, line them up and feed, change, bathe. Home time was baby time until bedtime. I truly didn't mind helping. I loved those kids like they were my real siblings, because in my eyes, they were. And being helpful instead of a handful made me feel like Dana and Bill would want to keep me around. 🤞

Please understand that I have such a sensitive heart. I truly didn't feel like anyone loved me or wanted me, other than Jack and Nappy. Two people who didn't have to. Two strangers. 😌

I joined the basketball team, of course. And track and field. Cross country. I met a great group of girls from my teams, and I mostly hung out with them around town and during school that year. Like I said, I was trying to avoid being home or being alone.

I was still actively attending the teen club and started going to clubs in other towns too. This is where I got close to my next friend. We'll call her Kathy. Kathy was sweet to me. Talkative. Very friendly with others. Super hyper. She attended all the clubs. We started going together. It was nice to not feel so vulnerable and alone.

She was quite known, and we were always surrounded by groups of people wherever we went. One night, we were at a club in Randolph. My parents were big on only driving one way, and Bill had brought us.

Kathy decided she wanted to leave with someone else, an older male. And she did. She didn't tell me. 🐵

Lesson #2: I will now prepare myself for two-way travel, regardless of people's promises.

Back to school, I was invited to the roller rink. I didn't get to do much as a child unless Jack brought me. The only time I had really been skating was at the park in Little Ferry before I was removed. This was a nerve-wracking situation for me because I just wanted to fit in. Sussex County was not like Bergen County. These kids were not friendly or nice. Judgment was always present. But I pushed through and went.

This is where I met my next boyfriend. We'll call him Henry. 🥸 🙏 Henry was a nice boy, raised right by a great family. Church folk. 🥸 They lived near the roller rink. He attended frequently with his friends and sister. His sister and I would become quite close after a few weeks. I started spending the majority of my free time out of town. Now, I was good. Safe. Off the market. We dated for quite some time, but between sports, the distance, and life, we separated. Always on good terms.

I would lose my grandmother Helen this year. 😌 I didn't get to attend the services, even though I had "family" across the lake, including my sister Marie's cousin, who I called my Aunt Lauren, and my cousins Denise, Fiona and Peter Jr.

Far right – My Grandma Helen ♡

To explain my relationship with them, I need to describe their relationship with each other. Aunt Lauren was my older sister Marie's cousin, Aunt Judy's daughter, and Uncle Donnie's niece. She lived in the basement apartment of the building my grandmother Helen owned in Edgewater while I stayed there after my arrival in New Jersey. Aunt Lauren and Uncle Peter had the kind of family and home I could only ever dream of. There was laughter, happiness, and love. I'm sure they dealt with life issues, but as a small child, I never noticed those moments.

My cousins Denise, Fiona, and Peter were always very close with each other. They had the kind of sibling bond I always wished I had. Out of all my siblings, I probably spent the most time around them, usually because I was being rescued by Aunt Judy and Uncle Donnie when things got rough at home.

Denise and Fiona would visit Aunt Judy during my brief summer stay, and I got to experience my first family vacation. Even though my reason for being there was for safety, it was a moment I had always dreamed of. My mother never did anything with us, and my relationship with my siblings was nonexistent. We weren't raised to be a family, to be sisters. We were raised not to exist, to shut up, sit down, protect ourselves, and figure it out on our own. The opposite of my cousins' upbringing.

I always envied their bond and their family, but never from a selfish or hateful place. It was more like a "do you have space for one more" kind of way. They didn't. I'm not sure why, but my cousins never treated me like their cousin. I say this from experience. I spent quite a bit of time around them and their other cousins, and they accepted them. But with me, it was different. They honestly never thought much of me, at least that's what their actions showed. Whenever we were together, it was them... and then me. Never us.

Right to left – My Uncle Donnie and My Uncle Tommy

41

I never thought much into it, because like I said, "family" was nonexistent. And everyone knew what was going on. No one saved me. No one spoke on my behalf, besides strangers. I guess it's easier to pretend a problem doesn't exist. 🧟 I seemed to be that problem. As if what I was enduring was deserved. 😔

I just wanted to be loved. To belong. Somewhere. Anywhere. But I never received that. At least not from this part of my family. I was a teenager by this point, with about ten years of being around them during the absolute worst moments of my life. The fact that I was purposely left out of my grandmother's funeral hit a different kind of nerve within me. I was filled with pain, resentment, anger, and sadness. My heart was slowly hardening.

I would also lose another important person shortly after this: Dana's dad, Dennis Connolly. Pops welcomed me as his granddaughter from the beginning. 🙏 ♡ I didn't get much time with him, but he had a good soul, and I'm grateful to have known him. I miss you both terribly.

Here we go, people. 😊 We're approaching some tea. ☕

As 9th grade came to a close, my perspective began to drastically shift. I was bitter. I was resentful, angry, sad, and tired. My soul was just tired. This was the year people could say I wasn't good to them, because I wasn't. On purpose. I was obnoxious, mean, a bully. I did anything and everything I could to get the hell out of there.

I never needed the things others did. I just wanted to belong. To have a family. To be safe. To be loved.

After everything that first year had shown me, on top of the move, losing my friends, Nappy, Jack, Shane, Pops, and now my grandma, and I couldn't even say goodbye to her? Every single person I loved was gone in a one-year span.

Dennis "Pops"

And I felt like I was just the live-in help until they decided to get rid of me. I wanted them to have a reason. I wanted to go back to Jack. Jack would have taken me to say goodbye to my grandma.

I was so bitter. I was hurtful. It was the absolute opposite of who I truly am. But I needed to become that person. I couldn't be who I truly am during this time. My heart couldn't take it.

And to anyone I hurt or treated poorly during this time, please forgive me. 🙏 You did not deserve that, and I am sorry.

I "dated" many boys this year. I just wasn't myself. A lot of older boys. Nothing lasted more than a few weeks. I kept it short and simple, basically ending things before any real connection could form.

In school, my grades declined. I didn't care. Like I said, I was on a mission. I had this teacher, Mrs. Carl, a Spanish teacher. I slept through her class and still managed to pass, just barely. Spanish was a no-go for me. It reminded me too much of my old life with Joyce.

Mrs. Carl exposed my truth as a foster child in front of my peers. It truly sent me into a spiral.

I also got my first suspension this year. There was a girl, we'll call her Mary, who told the principal I punched her. I didn't. I did nothing to her. But Mr. Princeton wasn't having it. He suspended me for three days.

I was pissed. He called Dana at work and told her I was suspended but would be allowed to finish out the day. It was maybe ten in the morning. After the call, he told me to return to class. I warned him not to do that because of how angry I was. He sent me anyway.

I walked out of the office and saw Mary standing outside the glass door with a smile on her face. I walked up to her, punched that smile right off, then turned around and walked back into Mr. Princeton's office.

My response?

"Now I punched that b*tch." 😂 😂 🙆

Five-day suspension. Worth it.

Girls never really liked me, through no fault of my own. It truly never bothered me. I was so used to being alone my whole life that I learned to love it. I love my own company.

And like I said, people love to talk. I let them. There's a reason I'm never confronted, only spoken about. Believe everything you hear, and leave me the hell alone. 😂 🙏

This year, I quit track and field/cross country. It was a fall and spring sport, which meant it was dark by six. I had about four hours of free time Monday through Friday before the kids got home from daycare, and I wanted more time for myself. I didn't tell Dana or Bill that I quit.

Dana found out when she attended a meet and my coach filled her in. Surprise. 🎉

Grounded. No phone. No AOL. No friends over. No going out. Just school and home. One month.

During this time, I was working at McDonald's in Landing, where I became close to my new best friend, Christine Meyers. We knew each other from school, but we got close through work. Christine lived a few blocks from me. She was a sweet girl with a big heart. I'm so grateful to God for bringing her into my life. 🙏 She truly was one of the best.

One day, a girl on the bus was picking on Christine. She was a grade or two older, and I honestly don't remember her name. I told her several times to stop. She kept pushing it. So, when we got off the bus, we had a fight. I broke her glasses, and she called the cops on me. 👮

I mean, I literally warned her. She made her choice. No reason to call the cops. I told her to stop, and that this wasn't the year to mess with me or people I cared about.

Christine and I became close quickly after that. She would be the girl I spent the rest of high school with.

This year, I truly formed a bond with Bill. Dana and Bill were opposites. Dana was more of a vocal enforcer, while Bill was more of a spiritual one.

I feared being punished by Dana. She had an angry look that could make you run for your life. 😠 She frequently raised her voice to show authority. Please understand, as an abused child, any type of loud, hostile, or displeased atmosphere puts me on alert. I don't deal well with raised voices. I'll avoid conflict at all costs.

45

Bill's way of punishment was making you feel condemned. 🥺🙏 He would say things like, "I'm truly disappointed in you," then give you the silent treatment until the punishment ended.

That was the absolute worst thing you could do to a child who already feels sorry for existing. But it worked. 🙏

This is when I met my next "lesson." We'll call him Derek.

Christine was dating Derek's friend, so by convenience, I started dating Derek. Both boys were older. Derek drove. We dated for about six weeks.

We broke up because I was turned off by his behavior. He would show up at my house without telling me and spend time with Bill. I told him several times that it was weird and that it bothered me. He didn't care, so neither did I.

Adios. 🙊

People must understand that once you show me that my feelings don't matter to you, it's a wrap. I learned very early in life that not everyone was like me. I know who I am and what kind of friendship or relationship you will receive while with me. Respectfully, it will never be my loss. 💯

This is when Bill starts teaching me things, basic life stuff relating to cars, the house, and people. We really start to form a bond where I feel wanted and seen. Bill was not one to say "I love you"; his love showed through his actions.

Home life is now run in shifts. 🥺🙏 Dana and Bill have multiple babysitters who shuffle in and out. The majority of baby time for me will be weeknights as needed and weekend mornings, from wake-up until whenever the sitter would come.

I'll get close to quite a few sitters over the next few years, but none that I chilled with outside my house. Still love you. 🥺🙏 Ally,

Maggie, Ariel. ♡ They experienced these periods of my life. All great women with very big hearts.

The kids are fun during this period. They are all walking, starting to talk. We spend a lot of time outside together. The kids were all very different in spirit. William was clumsy; everyone blamed it on his big head. Rose was a crybaby. 🫠 🙏 More of a screech. Mary was the adventurous one, always up to no good. And then Dennis, who was my favorite during this time. He was cute, talkative, friendly, and loved basketball. We would often take off, just me and him, typically to the park to play basketball or around town with my friends. ♡

This year, I will start working at ShopRite in Ledgewood. This is where I will meet my next boyfriend, who will also become my son's father: Charlie Shawl.

As 10th grade comes to an end, things start to settle down. I'm starting to feel like myself again, not angry or bitter. I'm back to my soft spirit. I'm happy again. I'm starting to feel like part of the family. I've really started to lay low and reflect on the things that I had done and the people I hurt during this time. 😞 🤦 I truly am sorry.

But because of this year, I will never allow my anger to overcome me again. Being the abuser was not for me. Being toxic was not for me. Acting out was not for me. I wanted to be the opposite. I wanted to be the light. To lift others. To help.

This year helped me realize that being soft and empathetic was not a weakness, but my strength. That love and forgiveness literally saved my soul from turning black. I'm not perfect, but I will make all future decisions with a little more consideration.

The summer between 10th and 11th grade was quiet. This will be the last time I EVER attend a club.

At the club in town, there was an older DJ. He was always nice to me, and I tended to hang around the booth a lot. He was maybe in his mid-fifties. On this specific night, he invited me downstairs. I thought nothing of it and followed. He had never given me a reason to question his intentions.

Me at the Club

Once I got downstairs, he exposed himself to me and told me to touch him. ☐ I left right away. I'll never step into a club after this moment.

We're maybe a month away from junior year starting. I'm still single at this point. A few weeks into working at ShopRite. This is where I will start to hang out with a new group of friends. We hung out in a group after our shifts, some from Hopatcong, others from nearby towns.

We filled our weekends with tag football or just hanging out. ♡ This group was safe. 🙏 They were all good people. So thankful to have known them all.

Darren, Mike, Richard, Melissa, Kristen, Dominic, and everyone else who was present during this time, thank you. 🙏

Chapter 4
Now What?

11th grade has arrived, and I am a different person. I start to officially date Charlie. He was quiet, older, and treated me well. I felt safe with him. This year was peaceful. No drama. No sexual harassment. Nothing too noteworthy other than me quitting basketball.

Now, the specifics to this situation were simple—the coach was a b*tch. 🙄 Not lying. She truly made the sport not fun for me. This was the year I realized I was safe and no longer needed it. It had truly been a safety net for me for a very long time.

Now, I wasn't going to talk about this during this chapter, but unless I'm completely honest, the choices I make because of this situation wouldn't make sense. Sorry it had to come out this way, but 🙈 honesty is key, and the only way we can help the next person is to own our stuff.

This is my absolute darkest secret. I have told zero people.

In the early spring of my junior year, I got pregnant. Now, I loved Charlie. I was ready to face this head-on. But he was older, by enough that it could have gotten him into trouble, even though we were right at the line of being legal. So, he thought it best not to keep it.

So... against my wishes... I had an abortion. 😔

Surprise 🎊 I'm not perfect. 🙈 I was young. I was scared. And I chose to follow the wishes of the man I chose to lead me. For those of you who feel the need to judge me or Charlie, I just want to remind you that neither of us gives a fu*k what you think. Best to tell your friends or neighbors how you feel. 🙄🙏♡

Because of this situation, I became at war with myself internally. I found myself praying for someone who would love me correctly, forever. 🙏 A constant prayer that played on repeat.

49

Mine and Charlie's relationship changed after this. I became more bitter and resentful. But I still stayed with him.

In July that summer, I found out that Charlie had joined the military. He never talked about it with me. I found out at his family's 4th of July party that he would be shipping out for boot camp come September. Surprise 🎉 Guess he was dealing with his own demons from what happened and decided running away would be the best decision. 🤷 Again... not the way you want to find out your boyfriend is leaving.

Now I'm on birth control. Taking it religiously since the situation. I never wanted to be in that place again.

September arrives. Charlie leaves. And that's that. Guess I'm dating long-distance now? We barely communicated during this period. Not sure of the specific rules, but he rarely called.

I start my senior year as usual. Keeping to myself like I have been.

Fall arrives, and I go to refill my birth control at Planned Parenthood, which was required every six months. I'd been taking it daily since the incident. Pregnancy tests were required before a prescription pickup. I wasn't concerned. Charlie had been gone a few months at this point, and I had been receiving my period.

As I'm sitting in the room waiting for my prescription, the doctor enters and tells me I am pregnant.

My first thought was that it was a joke. A hidden-camera type of situation. Like I said, Charlie was already gone for almost three months, and I hadn't missed a period.

I explain the situation and tell her that I haven't been active in months. I ask her to retest me. She decides to give me an ultrasound instead.

Surprise 🎉 I'm having a baby.

It's my senior year. I've done zero things to make sure my baby will be healthy. They tell me that my dates and the baby's size put me at an end-of-March due date: 3/31/2004.

It's December. I'm turning 18 in less than two weeks. Now what?

I'm panicking. The only thing I have going for me at this point is the fact that I didn't look pregnant at all. That will change within the next 45 days.

I already had plans to visit Charlie this year. He was now stationed in Pensacola, completing his training.

On December 26, 2003, I fly out to see him and tell him. He took it well. He proposes to me. Guess who's getting married? 🎉

I spend a week there before returning to New Jersey. When I return, I tell Dana and Bill the news. They take it better than I thought they would. Dana is super helpful, getting me scheduled for routine doctor visits and prenatal care.

It's now January. In the middle of the month, I'm pulled from school and placed on bed rest and home instruction. The next two months fly by. I am huge.

March arrives. I think that Charlie's parents are aware of what's going on and are just unsure how to deal with it, so I haven't heard anything from them. I finally get to talk to Charlie. He calls home, and I ask him why his parents haven't said anything to me about the baby or the engagement.

He informs me that he hasn't told them and that he will take care of it. 😔

I'm due at the end of the month. He calls them and leaves the good news on their answering machine. 🙀

They show up at my parents' store, where I've been working for quite some time. They explain that they just found out. I truly couldn't believe that they had to find out that way. 😤

The end of March comes. No baby.

April flies by... still no baby.

My doctor, Dr. Skoczylas, is an old man. Old-fashioned. He keeps telling me that the baby will arrive when he is ready. Doctors know best.

Here comes May. I arrive at my May 5 appointment, and I have had enough. 😔 I want this baby out. I'm vocal. The doctor finally caves. Schedules my induction for 8 a.m. on May 8.

I call Charlie. He flies home.

I arrive at the hospital with Charlie and Dana at 7 a.m. They get me on the table and insert the cervical gel. It's about 10 a.m. at this point. From 10 to 1... not much happens. But once 1 arrives, I'm in a lot of pain. The nurse suggests a warm tub. I climb in.

I must have fallen asleep because before I know it, it's 3. The doctor pulls me out of the tub, gets me on the table, and breaks my water. I climb back into the tub.

Again... I'm in and out. I am not medicated. No epidural. No morphine. I'm in pain, and my body keeps going to sleep.

6:15—here's my nurse. Ready to check me. Tells me to get out of the tub. I go to stand. Something is wrong. It's very hard for me to stand, and it feels like the baby's head is already coming out.

The nurse tells me I'm exaggerating. Finally gets me out and on the table. Two pushes later...

Here's my baby. 😍 ♡ 🥹

Jason James .

7 lbs, 5 oz. 21 inches long.

With a full head of hair and a big smile on his face.

I will never be alone again. 🙏 ♡

Jay was a good baby. He slept well, ate well, really, I have nothing negative to say about his arrival. Now, being a teen mom might have been scary for some, but I felt like God had been preparing me for this for a long time. 🙏 I had already helped raise five kids at this point. What was one more?

Graduation day arrived. I attended with my son in the crowd. ♡ School was over. That chapter had finally ended. Off to motherhood.

My Senior Year

Six weeks after Jay was born, I got into a pretty serious car accident. It was the only accident I have ever been involved in. We were both okay physically, but I totaled my dad's truck. That experience gave me a serious fear of being in cars, especially if I wasn't the one driving.

Jay's first year was rough. He had some pretty serious allergies to almost everything. I still wasn't driving. Dana and Bill helped me get around but were also very vocal about me getting back behind the wheel. No thanks. 🫣🙏

By September, Jay had a checkup. My parents were gone, and there was just a note next to the keys: "You're his mom. Figure it out." I cried all the way to his appointment, driving about 20 mph. But I made it. 🙏 Maybe it wasn't so bad after all.

Me and Charlie were still dating long distance. We were planning our wedding for December 26 of that year. Nothing big, just a small ceremony at his aunt's church where we were also going to baptize our son. The date was approaching quickly, and I was starting to feel stressed.

Jay was about six months old and having breakfast with my dad, which was a common bonding time for them. Breakfast and Friday or Saturday nights were when I would go by Bub's house to hang out after Jay was asleep. Bubby had become my best friend, and I frequently spent time at his house. This was really the only time I spent away from my son during his first year. Where I went, my son went.

While having breakfast with my dad, Jay had an allergic reaction. It was bad. We had to bring him to the hospital.

Surprise 🎊 Jay had a severe allergy to eggs.

I called Charlie. He was stationed in San Diego by then. He answered, told me he couldn't talk, and said he'd call soon. Then he hung up. Three weeks later, he called me back.

I was angry. I didn't care why he couldn't call. All I could think was that I'm supposed to marry this man in a few weeks, and he doesn't give a damn about me or our child. After we get married, I'm supposed to pack mine and my son's bags and move across the country with this man. This man who sees no fault in his actions. This man who is not acknowledging what I'm dealing with on my own.

And I guess the fear and disappointment I had inside my heart showed on my face. Because after a screaming match with Charlie on the phone, I hung up. My dad turned to me and said, "Lisa, you do not have to marry this man."

And I didn't.

I called off the wedding.

Charlie flew home for the baptism. We were still together, although our relationship was on the rocks, and we were trying to figure it out. Dana had been vocal about me not moving to California. She really felt it would hurt me to be out there alone without any help. So, I called that off too.

Instead, Jay and I went to visit Charlie in San Diego. This was right after Christmas. My first thought upon arriving was relief that I had a return ticket home. 😔 The only thing I enjoyed during the visit was the zoo. Jay and I spent the week by ourselves, only seeing Charlie for two days. The rest of the time, we stayed in the hotel. We flew home.

Over the next couple of months, Charlie and I talked less and less. I was very close with his family and friends, and so was our son. Family was always big for me. Growing up not loved made me want my kids to have love from whoever wanted to give it to them. I frequently visited all of Charlie's family members that first year of Jay's life.

Right to left – Rose, William, Dennis, Jay, and Mary on the Couch

I also need to make a special mention of a very special family that helped me and Jay during this year: the Castro family. Abuela, Melissa, and Amanda ♡ You guys helped me more than you can ever realize. I love you. Thank you. 🙏

Me and My Baby Sister May

May 8, 2005. Jay's big day. We threw a big party at my parents' house.

Guess who was nowhere to be found? Not even a call. Typical.

But... my baby sister was there. May.

I had driven down the shore to pick her up for Jay's birthday. This was where she had been living since we were removed. I believe this was her second home, but I'm not sure. She was 18 and dating. I hadn't seen her since I was 13. I was 19. I was so happy to have her back in my life.

She planned to stay for a few nights. We enjoyed Jay's day. I called Charlie. We fought. We broke up. Me, May, and Jay headed to bed.

At 1 a.m., I was awoken by my sister telling me that I had to drive her home right that second.

I was tired. I was scared of driving late. I begged her to tell me what was going on. She just said she needed to go. I called Bubby. He came right away. 🙏 Truly was my best friend. ♡

I loaded my son in the back with my sister, and we headed down the shore. We finally got there, and her boyfriend was waiting outside.

I was livid. I was under the assumption that I had to bring her home because she said that if she wasn't home, he would break up with her. A lie I wouldn't realize until after I blew up on him.

This man had no idea who I was. May had told everyone that her family had died and that her foster mother was her aunt.

My heart broke. 😭

In that moment, I realized that I no longer had a place in my sister's heart.

This was the last time I would ever see my baby sister. 💔

We leave. It's after 3 a.m. now. Me and Bub are both exhausted. He can't drive all the way back, so he decides we're going to sleep at Jack's and head back in the afternoon. I agree.

We get to Jack's around 4:30 a.m. Jack is asleep. The house is full, like usual. Shane and another kid are living in Jack's attic. A few local girls are sleeping on Jack's couches, and my old room is now someone else's room. There weren't many sleeping arrangements, either a futon with three people or possibly convincing the boys upstairs to share so I could steal one of their beds.

I set up Jay's playpen. He's out. Bub jumps on the futon with the girls and passes out.

Well... guess I'm going upstairs. 🙆

I head up. Me and Shane haven't spoken since I first got engaged. I'm arguing over the bed. He's trying to talk. After about two hours, I finally get some sleep. I'm up early, of course, but I'm exhausted. I'm ready to go home. I have work today. I'm working at Pathmark in Landing.

I finally get Bub up, and we head out.

Over the next few weeks, I'm frequently at Jack's. Jack has suffered a heart attack and is recovering. I have my own vehicle, which my dad cosigned for me. I'm working. I'm enrolled to start college come fall at CCM. My son is with me while I'm gone, except for a few nights when he stays with Charlie's family. I'm on the move, back and forth.

This goes on until June 21, 2005.

This is it. Let me just say this now: there is no animosity. The decisions that were made have been forgiven. There are always two sides to every story. You should believe them both.

I arrive home to Dana and Bill's. It was a Tuesday. I remember this only because I didn't come home Monday night. I had stayed at Jack's with Jay. Not a common thing for me to do on a weeknight, but like I said, I had been spending a lot of time at Jack's, typically arriving home late.

Once I walk in the door, I realize there's a problem.

I see mine and my son's things sitting by the door. My mom is angry. She's yelling. My room has been given away. She basically tells me to grab my belongings and go.

So, I did.

I will not speak to Dana for three years following this incident. I will speak to Bill a total of three times before he repossesses my car. Then I won't speak to him either.

It wasn't for any reason other than me feeling like their obligation to me was complete. I was nothing to these people, and they opened their doors for me when they didn't have to. Technically, I got an extra year more than I should have, and with my child. 🙏 I was grateful. No one owes me anything. They offered me safety for six years. 🙏

Now they had their own kids to worry about.

And I certainly wasn't helpful that final month at home.

As you've probably noticed, I haven't done a chapter rundown for the past two. It's simple: these lessons continue for quite some time.

Chapter 5
Where Do You Go When You Have Nowhere to Go?

So here I am, in my car, sitting in the Pathmark parking lot, hysterically crying. My son is in the back seat. What now, God?

As I sit there, all I can think about is what's going to happen to my son. I'll spend the next two weeks couch-hopping with Jay. Me and Shane will officially start dating on June 25, 2005. My reasoning is simple: Shane was my safe space. Since we were small, he always said, "Forever and always," and I believed it with my entire soul.

Shane comes into some money, and we finally get an apartment in Passaic. During this time, Jay is spending a lot of time with Charlie's family. I'm so grateful for you all during this period: Aunt Ann, Uncle Dave, Richard, Kaitlyn, Dee dee, Pa, and Gram. Thank you for being there for my son. It means more to me than I can ever express.

I withdraw my application for college. I lose my job at Pathmark. My car is repossessed. Jack gives me an Oldsmobile that runs, but just barely. I have to drive with the heat on full blast and pray there's no traffic. But it runs. I get a job working at Pascack Valley Hospital, and things start to look up for me. During this period, I reconnect with my sister Diane, who is now hanging around Jack's. She will also play a big part in my son's life for the next few years.

Joyce had just had triple bypass surgery, and me and Shane had just lost our apartment, so we decide to stay with Joyce. We don't have many options, and we all need some help. My first week there, I will have my first miscarriage. I'm 13 weeks. I'll spend the next two days in the hospital by myself.

My Mother Joyce

To give you an idea of the kind of person Shane was during this time, he was not someone to be proud of. He was a white boy who dressed like he was wearing a load of laundry four sizes too big. Fitted. Ego-driven. Prideful. Mentally and emotionally manipulative. Smoked marijuana. He was working with Jack delivering shoes during this time but basically spent his money on himself. This was okay with me. I was used to only God helping me out. I figured that out before Chapter 2. I just needed to feel safe, and his presence was enough.

So here I am at Joyce's. Me, Jay, and Shane. Joyce is still with Simon, but I don't remember him being there during these three weeks. I believe he was in the hospital with his own issues. Simon wasn't a man I wanted to be around, so I might have just blocked him out.

Jay is a little over two at this point. Talking, but not much. He's attending daycare at a church. On this specific day, Jay gets sick. I'm working at the hospital in Westwood. Joyce lives in Belleville. Jay's daycare is in Elmwood Park, which is the halfway point. Because I don't have a reliable car or anyone I can depend on down here, Joyce's neighbor is listed as the emergency contact.

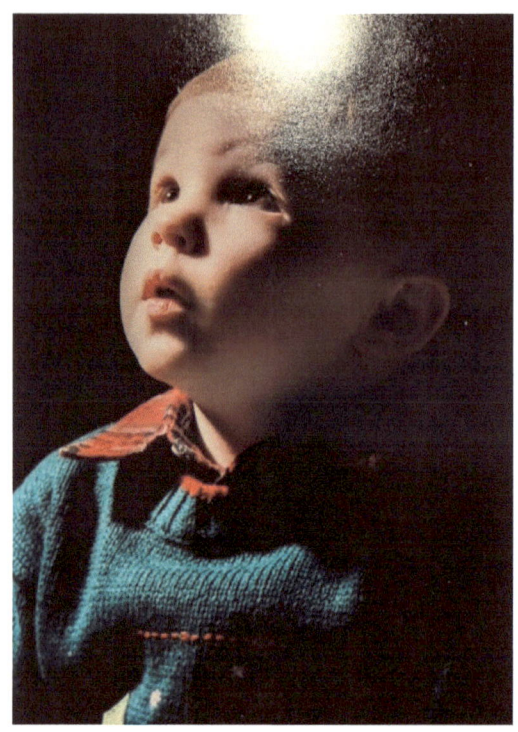

Jay

The school calls. She picks up Jay and leaves me a voicemail. I finally get it, leave work right away (I will be fired that day), and head to get my son.

I knock at her door, and she tells me he's with Joyce. It's been about an hour since she called, and I'm panicking. I'm getting flashbacks. It's probably about 2 p.m. now. Joyce just had surgery two weeks ago and was still recovering. She wasn't walking around yet, other than bathroom trips. I never suspected what I would walk into, given her condition.

But sure enough, I open her bedroom door, and she's smoking crack with my son at the bottom of the bed.

I'm heated.

How dare she do that to my son? How dare she invite that atmosphere into his life? I take my son, put him in his playpen in the living room where we had been staying, walk back into her room, steal ALL her crack supplies, and smash them in the street outside.

By the time I get back upstairs to get my son, she has already climbed out of her bed and is waiting for me at the top of the stairs. Joyce beats the crap out of me for the last time. She tells me that I am dead to her and that she regrets ever having me.

I respond, "I know."

Because I did, very early.

While gathering what I can, me and Jay leave. I press charges. This is the last time I will ever see Joyce until her funeral.

This is where God will once again show up on my behalf.

Me and Jay move into a battered women's shelter. This becomes our new home for the next eight months while I save enough money to move. We will be the longest residents in this shelter, where the typical allotment is 90 days. I enroll in a medical assistant program. I get a job with Kmart in Lodi.

The shelter is shared with other women and children. There are chores, curfews, and requirements that have to be met in order to stay. As you've probably figured out by now, the devil has been chasing me my whole life. This time period is no different.

I'm working at Kmart and I climb quickly in different positions over the next five months. I'm doing well in school. I'm saving money. Things are looking better. I'm hopeful.

Then, bam. Jay's sick. Really sick. In and out of the hospital kind of sick. We're running around doing tests. He's not sleeping, and neither am I. He can't keep anything down, can't go to daycare. This goes on for about a month.

I flunk out of school due to absences. Jay's got a problem with his esophagus and intestines. They do a colonoscopy and endoscopy. They remove some polyps. They change his diet and add more allergies to his list.

He slowly improves.

We will spend Christmas in the shelter with the other women and their children. 🙏 😌

Jay began spending a lot of time with my sister Diane, who had just given birth to my nephew Christian. She lived in the Bronx on Aqueduct Ave. She was the only person I had during this time. Shane was around… but only in spirit. 🤷 Shane never watched Jay. Ever.

I was finally promoted to Layout Manager. I was now making enough to start looking for a place. On February 22, 2007, me and Jay moved into our first apartment. We had no supplies other than what was donated from the shelter: Jay's crib, dresser, and some clothes. That first month was hell. I slept on the floor. Eventually, I saved up enough to get some furniture.

I was doing well at work. I was happy. Things were looking good.

This first apartment meant a lot to me. I had two neighbors while living there who would change my life: Donna and Tim. They were both older than me, maybe in their fifties. Donna lived upstairs and Tim lived in an apartment in the courtyard. He frequently visited Donna. Donna helped me more than she could ever realize. She couldn't have children of her own, but she treated me and Jay like we were hers.

Donna, and my lingering remorse over my abortion, would eventually lead me to donate my eggs. Surprise 🐣 I could possibly have 27 other children. (Don't worry, kids… my genes are stronger than my relatives') 👹 🤷 🙏

Me and Shane weren't doing well during this time, and I was contemplating leaving. I had emotionally connected with someone else. Shane was never much help and definitely wasn't nice to me. During this time, he cheated on me for the second time. I walked in on him at his cousin's house, doing the deed in a dirty closet. □

This will be the **only** time I ever have an STD: chlamydia. The proof is in the blood. 🤮 And the medical records. 🤮 Bet some of you are truly disappointed. 🙄 Not me though 🙏 I love rumors 🔪🤮

I was never one to cheat. Don't get me wrong, I connected with people during separation. (Don't worry, those deets will be unlocked as well. 🤮)

Back to my story. I was done. I'd had enough. I decided I didn't want to be with Shane anymore. He was never much of a partner. He was barely even my friend.

We're now at the end of February 2008. I had poured my heart out to the person I met at work, the old-fashioned way, through USPS. 🤮 We'll call him George. George was definitely my type. He also had a very nice way with words. He was no longer working there, and I hadn't heard from him for over two months.

Then he shows up at my job.

His feelings were reciprocated. He wanted to be with me. Take care of me and Jay. It had been two months; I had assumed he didn't feel the same, and I had already shut that door in my mind.

And now… plot twist… I was pregnant. Due in January.

I broke the news to him. Told him I had to try and make it work with Shane for the sake of our baby. He was upset but understood. He left. I would never see him again. Later, I would find out he was with someone else, and had his own baby on the way. 🙏

After this, I financed my first new car, a little red Tiburon. In May 2008, Bill, my foster father, reached out. He asked me to meet him for lunch at a local spot in Lodi. Me and Jay went. I hadn't spoken to anyone since they kicked me out and repossessed my car. He basically told me that he and Dana wanted me and Jay back in their lives. 🙏

So here I was, pregnant with baby #2, still working as Layout Manager at Kmart, still living in my first apartment in Lodi, trying to figure out how I was going to make it work with Shane. He hadn't changed much. He still wasn't much of a partner, friend, or provider. More of a placeholder at this point.

I was slowly starting to panic as time drew near. Before I knew it… we were in November.

Now, during this pregnancy, I had a lot of issues with my original doctor. Every time I went into her office, she told me I was four months pregnant and gave me a new due date. I had four different due dates, ranging from November 2008 to January 2009. I finally switched doctors in September. My new doctor, Dr. Reissman, was an older gentleman. He placed my due date in early December.

I arrived for my checkup on November 25, two days before Thanksgiving. After a rough exam, I began spotting. Dr. Reissman told me to go home, pack a bag, and head to the hospital. I was worried. I wasn't past my due date of December 8, and I was afraid the baby wasn't ready. The doctor assured me she would be fine, born over five pounds.

I went home, packed a bag, and told Shane. Shannon, Shane's mother, would accompany me during the delivery. We got to the hospital a little after 10 a.m. They started the Pitocin drip right away.

Within 30 minutes, I was in excruciating pain. This continued until a little after 6 p.m., when I begged for an epidural after they broke my water. I finally got one, some relief. I was in and out of it for the next few hours until the medication wore off. I woke up around 11.

This was it. The baby was ready.

Where was Shane, you ask?

Oh… he was outside in the parking lot with his cousin, smoking pot.

I sent Shannon out to find him.

Here I am… ready to push… but I can't push because everyone has left me.

The doctor finally enters, geared up. He tells me it's time. I start to push. But this one's different. This one's not easy. This one… I don't know if I can get out. I'm in excruciating pain. Shane and his mother arrive just as I deliver her.

Adriana Isabella has arrived.

4 lbs 13 oz, 17 inches long.

Something's wrong. She's blue.

They take her quickly to do her Apgar test. Then she's immediately removed from the room. I don't know what's going on. The nurse tells me they're running some tests.

We hear nothing for hours.

The complete opposite of Jay, who had spent every second with me from the moment he was born.

It turns out Adriana's lungs were not fully developed. She will spend the next 6 days in the NICU. I can only touch her through the glass. When she finally comes home… she's still unwell. She loses over a pound. I become paranoid that my breasts are suffocating her, so I switch to formula.

She spends Christmas at home.

We visit Dana, Bill, and the kids. This is the first time I'll see my siblings since 2005. They're now eight.

Adriana will return to the NICU on December 26 and stay until January 1. She was so small that even preemie clothes were too big. The preemie diapers had to be folded just to fit her. Other than her oxygen issues, she was a relatively healthy and happy baby.

Jason and Adriana

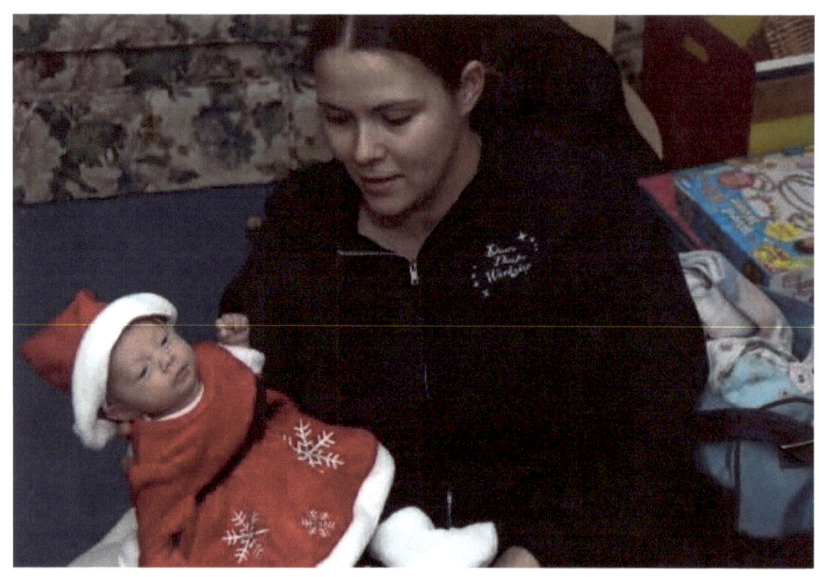

Me and Adriana at 1 Month – Her First Christmas at My Parents' House

This will be the last month we spend in our first apartment. We move across town to a second-floor apartment above Shane's family.

This is where I'll meet angel #5: Barbara Mastrofilipo. 🙏 ♡

Barbara was my landlord. Over the next year, we'll grow close, and she will become a strong support system for me and the kids. See... God always made sure me and the kids were good. 🙏 Without this woman, my life would have been a lot different. A thank you could never be enough. ♡

This new apartment was on the second floor of an old brick building with a two-car attached garage. It also had a reasonably sized yard.

This is the apartment where I'll begin my next chapter.

Because Adriana was born early, she was frequently sick during her first year with respiratory issues. She developed slowly, behind schedule, but she made progress. She started walking a little after one.

When Adriana turned 18 months, she began displaying unusual behaviors that raised some red flags for me as a parent. She would frequently smash her head into things and hurt herself, but it didn't seem to phase her.

When I asked the pediatrician about it, she told me it was age-appropriate behavior.

But I didn't accept that.

This was baby #7 that I got to raise.

This was not normal behavior for small children.

This is what I call flag behavior.

Adriana – When Her Behaviors First Began

Because of this, I started doing my own research on ways I could figure out what was going on with my baby. 🙏

Chapter 6
Who's Disabled?

After a few weeks of digging and doing some research, I found information on a place that screens children for disabilities. It was located inside Hackensack Hospital. The paperwork was excruciating, and the waitlist to be seen was ridiculous. Adriana was finally screened at the institute for child development when she was 2 ½. At this point, she was extremely active, and her behaviors were uncontrollable. They recommended she attend a local mental clinic that offers schooling and further testing for children who score below average. Adriana started attending school services at Passaic Mental Clinic when she was 3. She would attend school-like services for 1 ½ years before we officially received a diagnosis. Adriana is emotionally disabled. She has oppositional defiance disorder, dysregulation syndrome, ADHD, sensory processing disorder, and disruptive behavior disorder. She will continue to receive school services here until she enters a secondary program for disabled children in preschool.

During this period, Shane is non-existent. He is still living in the home but is not a parent, partner, or provider. He did not accept Adriana's diagnosis at 18 months and basically shunned her. ☹ I begin to seek outside assistance from other programs that could help Adriana. We screen for services through Bergen's Promise, and we are approved. She starts receiving in-home supports for behavioral therapy. I continue researching more assistance because Adriana's behaviors are continuously getting worse. Jay…my poor baby…spent many nights praying for his safety. No one helped me with Adriana besides my sister Diane, who now has 2 kids of her own and is still living in the Bronx. No sleepovers. No family help. Nothing. Her behaviors were absolutely uncontrollable. She would have bouts of rage where grown adults would be questioning their safety. My son slept with a lock on the inside of his door for his safety.

On a personal level, I have left Kmart. Once I returned from maternity leave, they had given my position away. I started working for Harbor Freight Tools. I was sexually harassed by the store manager and filed a formal complaint. I quit. Home life was hectic. When Adriana was two, we got our first dog, Max. I drove 4 ½ hours to the Maryland border to pick him up from a llama farm. ♡ This was right after Shane proposed to me. Surprise 🎊 guess who's getting married? It was a beautiful ring in the shape of a flower—small but meaningful to me. See, at this point, Shane and I had just reconnected. This was typically the ONLY time he was ever a partner…when I was ready to leave. I had one person in our lives who could control Adriana's behaviors from age 2-4. Miss Rich 😇 🙏 who was my best friend at the time. Rich would watch Adriana and Jay on the occasional night I would attend local bingo with Shane's mom, who lived below me with Shane's stepfather Ronald "Pop" and Shane's 4 brothers. Also, there were two "extended" brothers (not related but family regardless). Ronald's mother, Patricia "Nanny" Scotland, briefly moved in during this time. Nanny played a big part in my heart. ♡

She was a bitter old woman who was not afraid to tell you to go fuck yourself. 😇 🙏 Nanny was up there in years and needed some assistance taking care of herself. Shannon and Ronald were able to provide this for her for a while. But as time progressed, her care requirements became too much for them to handle, and I signed myself up for the services. Nanny came from a different generation. She believed in modesty and self-dignity, and anyone who has cared for an elderly person during these times knows that those moments are hard to come by. I, on the other hand, had been wiping butts my whole life 😇 and hers was no different. Whenever she needed me, I was there, with a smile, eager to help. I always tried to rebuild her self-esteem during those moments, but her being aware of her deteriorating condition truly saddened her soul. 😔 She was lonely and felt like a burden. 🏚 To me, she was the opposite. I looked forward to our moments together. 🙏 I'm glad I got to spend some of her final moments with her. You would be surprised what you can learn from the elderly, and quite frankly, they're the most honest. She was the first elderly person I cared for, but she will not be the last. I will also help my Uncle Donnie in his final days, who will briefly move in with my Aunt Lauren and cousins in Mount Arlington. I won't get long with Nanny before she passes, maybe a year total. Shortly after this, there will be discord in Shane's parents' home, and Ronald and Shannon will separate.

Patricia (Nanny) ♡

Shannon will move to Florida, and Shane's brothers will stay with Pop in Lodi and eventually move to Pennsylvania. During 2008-2013, the only people my son has are Charlie's family and Shane's younger brothers. Jay is basically handling his own battles quietly and beautifully. A battle he should have never endured alone. Although I never missed an event or game. 🙏 All of my energy and resources are going into getting extra care for Adriana and work, and Shane is being his normal self, doing whatever the hell he wanted. At this point, Shane had no responsibilities other than making sure he was good. He did not cook. He did not clean. The only time he interacted with his daughter was when he absolutely had to. He barely held a job. I carried us, like I always did. This year, we will move downstairs to the first floor. I will have a second miscarriage 😞 at 7 weeks. Other than Jay's sport activities, we attend no outside activities, no local parks, and have few home visitors.

Adriana's behaviors have peaked. This year, Adriana will have her first serious accident due to her behaviors. This will require her to have staples in the back of her head. This will also cause her second babysitter to have PTSD. 😢 🙏 Poor Lisa. Lisa was my neighbor. She was a gypsy woman (her words), a few years younger than me. She and her husband Mark lived upstairs after Pop moved, and she frequently watched a bunch of children. She was an absolute doll. We spent many nights swapping stories. ♡ Although she only watched Adriana by herself. Adriana had a serious issue with hurting other children still, and she had begun hurting herself as well. Adriana was being her normal self and was flipping around the house, and she fell upon the glass table and split her head open, gushing blood everywhere. I got home, loaded her and the hysterical sitter in my car, and headed to the hospital. I finally confronted Lisa in the emergency room regarding what happened. She responded that Adriana was doing flips and smashed the glass coffee table, still hysterical. I said, "Lisa… did you push her?" and she said, "Of course not," and I said, "Then why are you so upset? Accidents happen." She was scarred after that 😢 🙏 and never watched her again.

During this time, Miss Rich became homeless. I allowed him to briefly move into my basement so he could get back on track. While he was staying with me, my engagement ring was stolen. I found drug baggies in Miss Rich's room and had to ask him to leave. 😔 He was my best friend for quite some time. A very difficult decision for me, but ultimately it came down to the drugs. 😵 Simply couldn't have it around my kids. 🤷 I still love you, though, and pray you will help yourself ♡ which I'm sure he has. I started working at a local scanning company.

I began spending more time out of the home after this. Janelle, my best friend at the time, only lived a few blocks away. She had kids. One of her daughters was the same age as Adriana. Now Kenz… is a champ. 🫠🙏 She was an absolute blessing to my daughter at this time, and I truly feel that she helped change Adriana's heart. My daughter would do the absolute worst things to this little girl, and I would yell and say we were leaving. So… Adriana would run down a list of things she was sorry for… "Sorry for hitting, biting, kicking, yelling, pulling your hair… calling you ugly, blah, blah," and Kenz would be like… "Umm, you didn't pull my hair 🫠" and laugh it off, pulling her off to play again. This was Adriana's only friend. No one ever got along with Adriana. Not even her cousins (Bubby's kids). All involved were mean, except for Kenz. So grateful for this little girl's soft heart ♡. If Adriana didn't find Kenz, she would have spent the next 6 years without friends. Janelle was dealing with her own home issues, so we found comfort in each other, both at work and afterwards, with our kids. Where we went… they went. The men we chose for ourselves during this time… was us. 🫠🙏 We were the men in our families. The providers. The make-it-happen. The males who were holding space were added children. Suddenly, life got a little easier. We had each other to lean on. Her home became my sanctuary.

Adriana aged out of Passaic Mental Clinic and started attending South Bergen Jointure. This school required Adriana to be screened for medication. The psychiatrist prescribed Risperdal. We regularly attended psychiatrist appointments, and Adriana rarely slept due to her issues. She was prescribed additional medicine. ☺ Shane attended a total of zero doctor appointments with me. He had no idea what Adriana's conditions even were. I financed a new Elantra from one of Shane's friends, Eric Bennett (still the go-to guy).

So here we are, beginning of 2014. This is the first year DYFS will be called to my home. The worker arrives at my door. I answer. She explains why she is there. Someone said I was locking the kids in their rooms and not feeding them. Now, my son was on the smaller side growing up but was healthy. Very involved in sports, so he had an athletic body type. He's 9. Adriana, on the other hand, was the opposite. She was experiencing a reaction to her new medication and was heavy. I allowed the worker in… allowed her to see the kids… their rooms… the home. I explained that we were heavily involved with state services and that clearly there had been a mistake. State services require mandatory reporting if abuse or neglect is suspected. I had voluntarily signed myself up for help. She explained it was a mandatory 6-month case. 😔 Great.

Adriana was still receiving in-home support services. She was still uncontrollable. This year, I was told that my landlord would be selling her home. 😔 I began to panic. My daughter's behavioral therapist offered to rent me her home in Montague. During this time, I was still employed with the scanning company which I commuted back and forth to on the weekends and the occasional overnight. Adriana started school at Northern Hills Academy. During this time, I still had an active DYFS case. Shane was still living with me and had been ordered to attend rehab services for marijuana. Me and him were struggling to make things work. He also proposed to me for a second time with a larger ring. This was his way of shutting me up. It always came down to material things for him. In his eyes, it was a replacement. The ring meant nothing to me. I wanted the promises that should have come with it. Who stays engaged for 8 years?

February 2015. I'm awakened to a phone call from my sister, Diane. It went like this: "Hello? Mom's dead." And that was that. Now, I haven't spoken to Joyce since court. Well… since the beating where she said I was dead to her. It's 3 a.m. Why the hell am I hysterical over this woman? This woman who was responsible for everything that I had endured. I should be cold. Heartless. Like she was. But I was truly crushed. 😔 See... in my eyes, she was going to figure it out. Stop the drugs. See what she could have and fix it. Apologize. Show up. Be a damn mother. I didn't ask to be born here. I didn't ask for the life she provided. Which was null. How dare she just die? Of course, the funeral was on me. Diane could not hold a job. She rarely had money unless John gave it to her. She was also struggling with her own addictions at this point. Percocet. I plan the arrangements… pay the bill. I will then be required to empty her belongings from the building she was living in. By myself. So, here's the end… everything has been completed. I can finally close this chapter. But apparently, Simon was under the assumption that I was going to step in and make sure he was good afterward. I truly tried to help him set up services for himself through welfare. He is probably in his 70s at this point. But that man… who took my mother from me… who beat me… who allowed the absolute worst to happen to me… deserved nothing from me. And he would call… and ask me to buy groceries… and pay his bills… and take him to the doctor. And I did… for a little bit, but I just couldn't continue to pretend to be okay when I wasn't. And when I tell you that I had to change my phone number and ghost him, I'm not lying. You and what happens to you, Simon… is between you and God. 🙏 And your kids. Call your own damn kids. Who you protected by staying the hell away from. 🤓

Simon

77

March of 2015, my Elantra will be repossessed for non-payment for the 3rd time. This will be the same day I come home to no electricity for failure to pay. I had been working at the scanning company still and had been traveling back and forth. I had given Shane money to pay both, and neither were paid. I will call my dad and beg for a loan. He will tell me that he cannot help. Anyone who knows me… knows how hard this moment was for me. I am not one to ask anyone for help. Besides God. I will apply for a personal loan on the Internet and will be approved. The following day, I will have power and my car back. This situation will cause me to break up with Shane. Because what? You just going to steal my money while I'm killing myself trying to keep us afloat?

April, I will receive my first letter from DYFS that I am an okay mom. 😅 I will inform my landlord that I will not be renewing my lease and will be leaving on August 31st. Adriana will be hospitalized again and diagnosed with a new disability. An unknown seizure disorder. Now during this year in Montague, a lot has changed. Adriana's original psychiatrist has been booted. Adriana had gained so much weight from her medication that I had become concerned about her health. When I confronted the doctor, her recommendations were to increase the medication I was concerned about. 😕 That night… I pulled Adriana off all of her medication. 🤦 Absolutely the worst thing that you can do. This will cause a psychotic breakdown, and she will be forced to stay inpatient for a week. We will also receive a new doctor. Dr. Edward Hall. 🤍🙏 This doctor will change Adriana's life. He will prescribe different medications more suited for her behaviors. He will be our doctor until Covid.

Adriana and Jay – Right Before She Was Placed Inpatient

The home we were staying in during this time had a full glass front. Floor-to-ceiling windows. It was a fairly decent-sized home. The bears frequented our trash. 🚲 This house did not go above 50 degrees in the winter. In any room. The windows were not tempered, and the baseboards were directly below the windows. There was a small wood stove. The living room was the warmest room. Anyone who knows me… knows this is a no-go. I was sure I would freeze to death in this home. 🚲 🙏 But… I made it. Happiest day of my life, driving away. When I leave this house, I will briefly live with Dana and Bill on their dining room floor for 3 months.

Winter Thermostat in Montague

Chapter 7
Time to go home

My main reason for moving back to Hopatcong was because my dad hadn't been feeling well. I only saw them on holidays or when I would come up to clean. Just call me Consuela. 👺 🖌 Between working almost 2 hours from my home, and being an hour from Hopatcong, moving made the most sense. Bill had been in and out of the hospital quite a few times at this point and I wanted to be closer to him. To everyone. So... we made the dining room work. Finally... move-in day. I will move into my first house in Hopatcong. I will pick up a 2nd job at the deli. I am no longer with Shane I am seeing someone from my job in Lodi. We will call him John. John... was the opposite of Shane. In every aspect. Totally not my type at all but boy was he funny. 🤭 I never worried about my safety with him. Although I wouldn't refer to our relationship as strong. More like a close friend with perks who you rarely see or talk to. 🤭 He was a good guy. Honestly... we didn't work out because I truly felt like he was still in love with his ex. So, I was never really open to giving him my all. He invited me to his mom's birthday party, and I didn't go, so we broke up. I will find out I'm pregnant shortly after we break up. He will date someone else that works with us. I will miscarry for the 3rd time. I took this one hard. There was just so much going on at this point, I wasn't sure what to do with my life. This will cause me to retreat to my old patterns.

Me and Shane will briefly reconnect. 😵 I get it people... I'm tired of me too... 🤭🙏. I will get pregnant... again. During this time, Shane will confront Bill about the pregnancy. Bill was an emotionless man. You could never truly know what he was feeling on the inside. But he was not a fan of Shane. Or the parent he was to Adriana. Or the partner he was to me. He was big on the 3 P's. Spoke to me often about it but I think I took it too literally and became them. 🤭 He

81

would always tell me "Lisa, a man has 3 jobs. Please his wife, protect his family, and provide. Without that… you have a woman." 😛 Am I a lesbian? 😵 Shane tells Bill he plans on stepping up to the plate and finally taking his position to lead our family. I will leave the deli when I find out I'm pregnant. At this point, I am still traveling back and forth to my job in Lodi. My best friend Janelle will move to Hopatcong from Garfield. Adriana will have her 2nd extended stay at Bergen Regional (yeah yeah… Northbridge… IDC… it will always be Bergen Regional to me) 😵. Things will slow down. Shane will get a decent job. Adriana is doing well behaviorally thanks to new medication. She has dropped a ton of weight.

Jason and Adriana – His Foot Injury Upon Arriving in Hopatcong

Jay is now in high school. No longer involved in sports. Jay had a very terrible transition into Hopatcong. When we first arrived, he was fairly liked. But he had a pretty serious leg injury during football season and things took a horrible turn. A lot of rumors were spread about him. Jay was always a good boy. But he was bullied so severely that he will have his own visit to check his mental health out. He will attend Lenape for the remainder of his schooling.

When I am 5 months pregnant, things will start to get weird. My landlord will start allowing people onto the property and into my home without my consent. The final straw will be me coming out of the restroom to the landscaper (male) in my home. I will call Bill hysterical. He will help me find another home 3 blocks away. We will move when I'm 7 months pregnant. December 2017. During this time, I am stressed. I'm super pregnant. High risk. Naturally because of Adriana's birth and the miscarriages. I will also undergo genetic testing during this time to see if Adriana's health problems were genetically created. They were not. I carry no markers for any gene mutations. Adriana was born premature. 😵 No shit. This was not new information for me. Her being born in respiratory distress told me that. But apparently, not missing Thanksgiving dinner was a more important reason to force her out. So grateful she made it. ♡ She is the reason I learned to use my voice. 🙏 This beautiful child who is now flourishing at 10 years old. This child who doctors recommended "in" facility placement for and referred to as a lost cause. This child who has fought for her life every second of her life. Both physically, mentally, and emotionally. She is my whole world. This child whose life has been nothing but continuous doctor appointments and tests. Is finally doing well. So grateful for everyone that helped Adriana during this transition. Special shout-out to two special women who taught me how to fight for my child during this time. Ms. Andrea Romano and Mrs. Alyssa Summer. 🙏 I couldn't have done it without you two. Even after we left… you fought for us. Angels. 😇 These women will help me transition Adriana into public school.

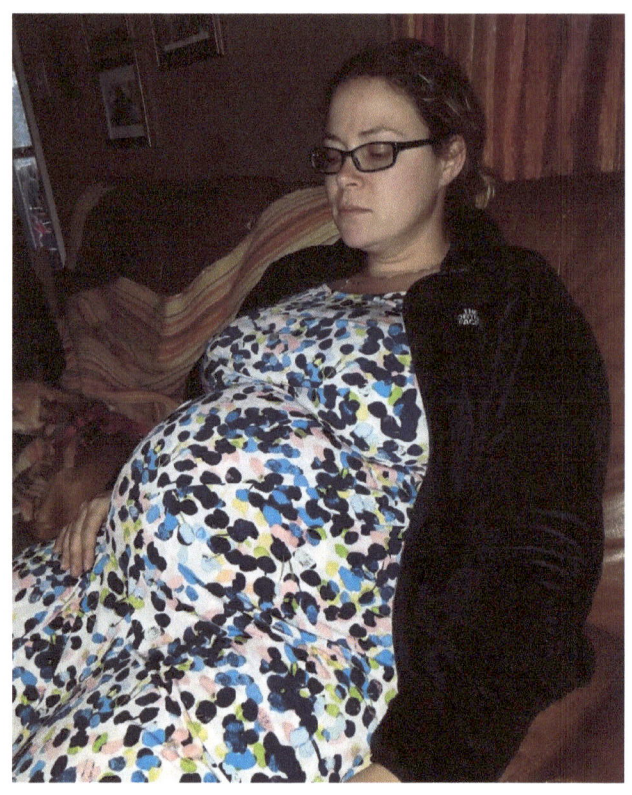

Me Pregnant with Avery

We have now arrived in January 2018. My baby's due the 31st. I'm scheduled for induction on the first of February. This was recommended because I had never gone into labor naturally. This was baby number 3. Surprise baby. My rainbow baby. I want to have a water birth. After my last one… I want as little stress as possible. February is here. I arrive at the hospital bright and early. 8 a.m. The doctor comes in. Says good morning. Settle in for a long day… I'll see ya later and heads out. 10:30 a.m. they come in… start the drip. I want to go natural this time. Like Jay. No meds. About an hour passes. I'm uncomfortable. I want to go in the tub. I'm at Newton. It's not as nice as Hackettstown. Or Englewood. It was just an open room and an inflatable tub. I call the nurse. She's a b*tch. Tells me it's too early. I must stay on my back. I'm so uncomfortable. I really try to push through it. 12:15 p.m. I am over this fu*ken nurse. 😤 😠 I am in a lot of pain, and I have pushed the button like a million times. She's taking her sweet ass time. Finally arrives. I tell her I want to go in the tub. It's only me and Shane in the room. She calls me a crybaby and gives me a morphine shot through my IV. I tell her I need to push. She laughs me off. I get really angry and tell her again that I need to push. She lifts my gown and yells "Omg don't push" and screams for the on-floor doctor. I tell the nurse fu*k you. 😤 Because for real. The on-floor Dr, Dr. Abdullah arrives, and she is still trying to gown up. Baby's almost out at this point. She now has her hand on my baby's head trying to stop her from coming out. One push and she is out. Dr. almost drops her. She hands her right to me. Morphine has just kicked in… Here's Avery Jade, 7 lbs 8 oz, 22 inches long. Here, Dad. Momma's going to bed.

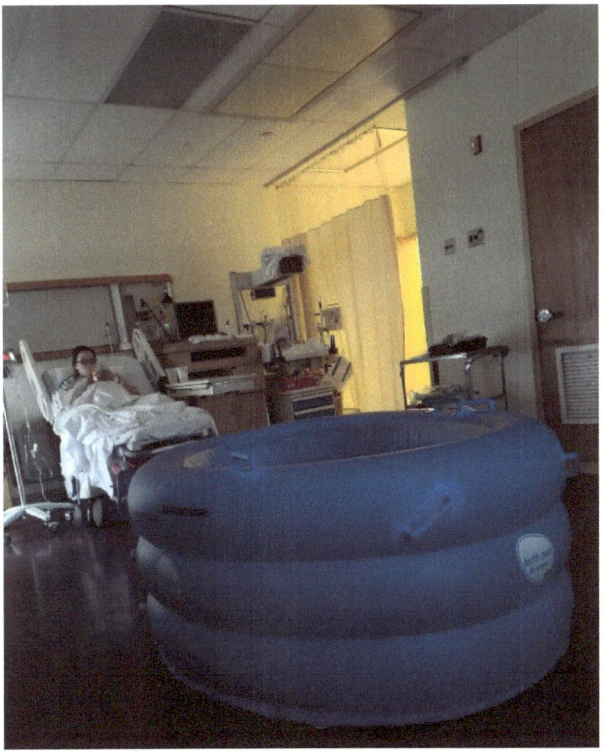

Me Awaiting Avery's Arrival – And the Tub I Never Got to Use

When I wake up about an hour later… I'm mad. Mostly because I didn't get to have her in the tub. And I had a whole lot of not-so-nice things running through my head on what I wanted to do to that nurse. My doctor shows up around 4 to meet my baby. 😔 Too late now, doc… should have stayed. I mean it was less than two hours… 🙊

This is where Shane's heart will change. Shane never wanted to be a dad. He didn't have one growing up, and the ones that were around did not treat him well. He was a for-show partner/father, if that makes sense. Wanted the perks of being present but never wanted to put in any work. Although this is his second child, this was truly his first. They had a very special bond. Shane truly stepped up to the plate once Avery was born. With Avery.

Although I was so happy for Avery, I couldn't help but be sad for Adriana. This is the relationship she should have had with her dad. But she didn't. She truly only had me. Shane is still working. He's helping around the house. Finally helping me pay some bills. Things are going ok. Adriana is excited about her baby sister. Her and Jay did not have the best relationship. Pretty sure it was the constant threats to take him out, but 🙊. Her behaviors have become almost nonexistent at this point. 🙏 We have finally found some medication that helps. Her school is still going well. We are good.

Avery and Our Dog Max – Right Before I Got Sick

Almost 6 months to the day after giving birth, I will wake up to the most excruciating stomach/abdominal pain. July 31, 2018. The day that will change my life. This will continue on a daily basis for about a week before I take myself to the doctor. They give me some pills… say I need to follow up with a gastroenterologist. From August to November 2018, I spend almost every day in excruciating pain. I finally get into the GI specialist. Now at this point, I'm pretty heavy. Starting weight in July was 258 lbs. I was a size 24. Because of what I have been dealing with internally, I've dropped about 30 lbs. Not too bad. Specialist runs tests. Gives me an endoscopy/colonoscopy. Says I have severe inflammation. Diagnoses me with IBS. Gives me medicine and sends me home.

For the next month, I take these pills. They do nothing for me but give me acid reflux.

To give you an idea of the person I am during this time, it would be one that you don't want to be around. 🧟 And people didn't want to be around me. I became miserable. I complained a lot. I wanted to be left alone. I felt like people had no sympathy for what I was enduring. They were uncompassionate. They just wanted me to keep showing up to cook, and clean, and fix everyone's problems and I literally could not. I didn't even feel like myself. 🙁 I was miserable, and I truly felt like I was losing my mind. From August to December, I only had my dad. He spent many nights listening to me cry. 🙏

I honestly did not have a close relationship with Bill until I moved back to Hopatcong. Although he was the one who spent the most time with me.

January 2019. I have returned to the gastroenterologist. Tell him his pills suck. He tells me it's in my head. 😤 The freaking nerve. Ok, doc. I'll play your game. Let's see if you're right. So… I sign myself up for some therapy.

Here we go doc… what's wrong with me? Give it to me straight. I can handle it. Just not the pain that I have been experiencing. 🤕 A little PTSD… little anxiety… little depression. Whole lot of "not nuts." These were all reasonable things relating to what I was experiencing. Minus the PTSD. Clearly that came from my earlier years. To wake up one day and suddenly not be yourself would give anyone anxiety and depression. Recommendations? Lexapro. Continued therapy. Suggestions? New GI doctor. I take their recommended "drugs." I will receive notice that they will be selling the company that I have been working for. They will close in 23 days. 😣 February arrives, and I'm over the pills. So, I start to go to every other day.

March. I am not myself. Me and Shane are not good at all. You see, since I've been sick, Shane had to step up and be me. Not so easy, huh? I literally was just trying to make it through each day. Nothing extra. Absolutely nothing. I did not cook. I did not clean. I could not eat. I spent most of my time crying and complaining in my bed. I truly was a different person. I have poured my heart out to Shane. I ask him to help me. I explain to him that I am not myself and I need him to be my partner. He ignores me for 5 days. Literally 👋 not 👋 a 👋 word.

Now I have never been one to snoop through anyone's things. Just not in me enough to care. People cheat. People lie. People hide shit. These are facts. Learned them early. And if you don't care to do right by me, me snooping and complaining is not going to fix that. So, I never bother. Again, I have only ever had him in presence. I never had Shane's passwords. What he did was his business. But he left himself logged in on my laptop, which I rarely used. And I happened to come across quite a few things that caught me off guard.

Shane had spent the previous night at a bar with an old female friend from school. Again, not an issue with me. He frequently hung around women. I've never been the jealous type. You're not me, and I sure as hell... don't want to be you. 🙈 I love who I am. Always have.

But this specific conversation included searching for how much child support he would have to pay if he left… how I did nothing but take up space… how he didn't find me attractive… how he did everything… yeah (for 5 months because I literally could not)… how he didn't love me. 💟 🙆

I sacrificed so much for this man. I stood by his side. I stayed after he did me dirty time and time again. I built him up and encouraged him to grow. I wanted us to make it. I was far from perfect, but I was true to him and our family. And I'm nothing?

My whole life I'm chasing safety and sacrificing for a man who can't stand me? What the fu*k am I doing? When I tell you that I was destroyed in a moment… I am not lying. I gave this man on and off 15 years of my life. More like 25 if you count our childhood. I always thought he would be the one. Just like Joyce, in my mind… he would realize what he had… and change.

When he walked through my door, I was knee-deep in my daughter's room cleaning. 🧹 This is my go-to during crisis. The cleaner my home… the sadder I am. I will scrub my home with a toothbrush if I need to. 🫤 Definitely a trait I carried from childhood.

You can tell I've been hysterical. But I am calm. He walks in my daughter's room. I hand him his engagement ring back. I tell him to pack his things and to get out of my house. He asks me what's going on. I repeat my request and tell him he already knows. He then tries to flip things on me (typical narcissistic behavior with him). When he sees that this isn't playing out in his favor, he tries one final attempt to self-plea the pity aspect. Like I said. I have been broken. I did not care. This man is the devil. I tell him that.

In that moment… I am lighter. He grabs his trash bag of clothes and leaves. Pretty sure he moved in with his cousin but 🤷. I didn't care. Goodbye, Satan. ☠️ I'd rather die alone than next to a demon playing in my face in my lowest moments.

So here I am… single… 3 kids… super sick and now alone in every aspect. Now what?

Chapter 8
Time to figure it out

I struggled the first couple of weeks. I questioned my decision on leaving Shane. You see, Shane consistently let me down. Our whole lives. It was his thing. My thing was forgiving and forgetting. Every time. But like I said, this time was different. I have never needed anyone in my life. I have never poured my heart out and asked someone for help. It's never been my thing. I learned early that the people who will help you, you won't have to ask. But I did. And his response destroyed my soul. It could not be forgiven. It could not be forgotten. Not this time.

During this time, I don't have many people. My friends... my family... have all left me to myself. No one likes when people are down and vocal. I got my dad, and I got another close friend from my old job, Nikki. She was pretty much the only person who could stand me at this point. 😬 Thanks, Nik ♡ 🙏 this is when I will attempt the whole "dating" thing.

Being outside of the real world for 15 years was like walking out into the wild. What's this online dating crap? What the hell? This is the new cool? Yikes. Ok, let's give it a go... few dates out with some random dudes, quickly helped me decide this wasn't for me. Apparently, if you go on a date, the expectation is a trip home with you. 😳 Umm, what? Sir... you don't even have a job. And because of my past, I was never promiscuous. I'm a very selective person. Typically, bad choices 😬 ... but not many. I've always been a long-term kind of woman. When I am with someone, I'm with someone. Sex was a chore unless I was interested. Not something I was out seeking. I was seeking safety and peace. After 2 failed attempts at finding someone to hang out with, I quit. Online dating was not for me.

Out of nowhere, I will reconnect with someone else from my past. We will call him Israel. Israel was on house arrest. 🤐🤖 Not my business. Like I said... I knew him from childhood. We both grew up rough and I'm not one to judge. He was nice to me. He wanted to spend time with me. These were the things I wanted at this time. And I needed to stay clear of Shane. So, Israel filled this spot. I frequently visited him for about 3 months. We really got close. I didn't need a label, but at this point, I am assuming that we are both on the same page with each other's company. Boy, was I wrong. I will pop by his house randomly one afternoon. His house will be filled with young girls. At least 4 that I can recall. I enter. I'm sitting on his couch. It's loud. Complete 180 of the typical atmosphere. Everyone is going in and out of the restroom. 😵‍💫 Taking turns. Again... I'm just sitting and observing. Clearly, it was drugs. I'm used to this sporadic behavior from my childhood. This is my typical response. Observe silently. Suddenly, I am called into the restroom by one of the girls he has over. I walk in. There's another girl inside. We will call her Alice. Alice informs me that she's seeing Israel. 🐵 And will be "staying" with him for a while. This is a common thing with women and me. Everyone feels the need to humble me. They don't come more humble than me. 🤚 My response? Oh… okay. 🤖 I leave. I don't say anything to Israel. I basically stop reaching out and he doesn't care to find out why, so it dies out. Probably best. Good luck.

Diane and her 3 children will briefly move in with me. I will receive a phone call that John has left her and the children on the side of the highway in the Bronx, and they will have nowhere to go. During these 3 weeks, I will find her a job in town. 🙏 I will help her start the paperwork to enroll the children in school. I will watch her kids while she is working. I will try and help her get on her feet. Stand on her own. Learn to depend on herself. 🙏

During this time, I will find drug baggies in Adriana's room. I will confront my sister. She swears she's no longer taking pills. Although she frequently displays evidence that she is under the influence. Diane had frequently stolen things from me and my children over the years to feed her addiction. Mostly electronics, money, and jewelry. Material things that never mattered much to me. When questioned, she would pull either the pity card or go into denial. But this time, she will try and tell me that it's makeup. 😵 Say that I'm imagining things. I will lose it. I will publicly embarrass her outside of my home in front of my neighbors. 😣 I will tell her she is just like Joyce and that she needs to leave my home. I will offer my nephews and niece the option of staying with me. They will decline and leave with my sister. This will be the last time I see my sister Diane or the kids. The last I heard, she had left her kids with John and took off with a new boyfriend. 😔 I'm truly sorry for my niece and nephews. Wish she was strong enough to break this family curse for them. But sadly… you cannot help someone who does not want help.

I will spend the majority of my summer with Nikki. We frequently stay up in Pennsylvania with Pop. Pop's got a beautiful home on a quiet lake and Shane is watching the children on the weekends at my home in Hopatcong. He is still living with his cousin at this point. My kids were not allowed at his cousin's house. Now CJ (Bub's brother) was a great guy to me. We always got along well, and he treated all of my children like family. CJ was young. CJ did not clean. His living space was not an appropriate atmosphere for children. This is probably the only thing that me and Shane were on the same page about during this time. We are still not getting along. There is a lot of animosity over the fact I haven't forgiven him yet. At this point… I'm probably about a size 16. Down about 50 lbs. Still suffering from unexplainable stomach/abdominal pain. Still questioning how much time I truly have left. I was just in a very bad place mentally. I was truly starting to feel like I would pass at any time. This summer I will really reflect on my life. The things that I have endured. The things I had survived. Just to be taken out by man-made problems. This was definitely the lowest point in my faith. The only time I ever questioned if I was alone. 🙏

Me and the Kids – Roughly 220 lbs.

August has arrived. I'm up at Pop's. Like usual. Like I said, I was over the dating scene. I was just looking for a little peace at this point. And I love hanging solo. I have basically been alone my whole life. I finish a delicious spaghetti and meatball meal. 🍝 I'm heading out from using the bathroom. Something is wrong. I feel like I am burning up from the inside. My body feels heavy. Heart feels like it's pounding. Sharon "Nana" is standing in the kitchen, sees me, and says I don't look well.

Shit... I don't feel well.

Sharon and I have known each other for quite some time now. She was a close friend of mine from Lodi. She treated me like her daughter. She endured parts of my story with us. 🙏 Her son and my son were best friends. She was a strong support system for me and Jay. ♡ Especially Jay. She was like a second mom to Jay when Adriana's behaviors were at their peak. He will attend many sleepovers and trips with her. I'm so grateful for all she did for us. 🙏 Love you forever.

When I wake up, I'm in the ambulance. I have no idea what is going on. I'm in and out of it for the whole trip. I arrive at some hospital in Scranton. They got me hooked up to a whole bunch of things. I'm starting to feel better. A team of doctors come in. They ask me what happened. 🤷 Beats me. All I know is I didn't feel well and now I'm here. They spend the next 24 hours running all kinds of tests. Asking all kinds of questions. I will spend a total of 4 days here while they try and figure out what's going on.

I had just returned to work at this point. Another scanning company in Andover. I was on unemployment since the end of March. The doctor comes in and tells me that my body is attacking itself. He suspects that I might have NCS. Neurocardiogenic syncope, now known as vasovagal syncope. The precursor to POTS. This was 2019, so way before it started being cool.

With this condition came other side conditions. Bradycardia, extremely low blood pressure, inability to regulate my body temp, and basically my brain telling my heart that I'm dead. And I get to pass out. Fun fact: sometimes, people with POTS never pass out. They only get the extreme dizziness and can redirect it. 🖐 Was not one of the lucky ones. All on top of the unexplainable stomach pain I have been enduring since the previous summer 🎊 Yay.

September/October 2019... just call me miserable. 😔 I spent this time mostly with Bill. Bill was always fixing or making something, and I needed to be busy. He was the only person who truly had sympathy for me. He was dealing with his own autoimmune disorder and was frequently being admitted as well. At this point, I barely have any friends. Summer is over. People were over me complaining and kind of forgot about me. 😠 My children, Shane, my siblings, my friends, and even Dana were vocal about me being a miserable person to be around. 😞

Well, I'd sure like to not be sick if that helps anyone feel better?

At this point in my sickness, I was passing out a few times a day. I frequent the emergency room. My children are now directing my life. No locked doors, no showers, walking in front of me down the stairs. 😠 I'm now seeing a cardiologist. They recommend a heart monitor and more tests. Now, there's no medication or cure for POTS. They offered me Midodrine, basically the only medication to show improvement for my symptoms. Although it didn't help much. Other recommendations? Basically, increase my salt, stay hydrated. Pray for the best.

Me and Shane are still separated. He sees the kids on the weekends at my house. So, since August 2018, I have been diagnosed with 7 different disorders: IBS, anxiety, depression, PTSD, NCS, bradycardia, and low blood pressure. In my head, I am dying. This is what I am physically and mentally feeling.

What the hell is going on?

This was the only thought that was running through my head. I am down about 75 lbs since I originally got sick. Now sitting around 180.

November 4th. I get a call that will destroy my whole world. Again. It's Dana. Bill's had an episode. Passed out. He's on his way to the emergency room in the ambulance. Dana is heading down behind them. It's a Monday night. Shane is still living with his cousin in Carlstadt. I ask him to come stay with the kids so I can meet my mom at the hospital in Dover.

I head to the hospital. It's probably a little after 7 pm when I arrive. They have already called my mom into the consultation room. 😔 Once I realized this, I knew I would never see my dad again. Bill's heart had stopped on the way to the emergency room. They got it restarted. But he never regained consciousness. Brain dead.

Me and Dana will spend about 3 hours just sitting outside of his room. My dad took care of everything for my mom. 😣 I can't imagine what was going through her head during these moments, but I'm glad she wasn't alone.

We finally head out. Dana invites me for some food. I decline. Only because Shane was at my house with the kids. He's got about an hour to get home, and I don't want him to have to stay any longer. I head home.

Once I arrive, Shane will be in my bed. All ready to stay for the night. I walk in my room, tell him about my dad, thank him, tell him that he can head out. We have been separated almost 8 months, and I haven't caved on forgiving or forgetting. Shane responds with hostility. Says I'm a piece of shit for asking him to leave so late after he drove all the way up just for me. Says I am selfish.

Ok. Thank you. For being a parent. Please leave. 🙏

For the next four days, I will have to keep what I know to myself. My brother and sister were away at college, and my mom wanted everyone to come home before anything was said. I am not a good pretender.

November 8th. We will all head to St. Clare's Dover hospital. Nothing has changed. Bill is still hooked up to life support. We spend a few hours with him before they move him upstairs to hospice. From the time he arrives at hospice until his death, it was a total of about 20 minutes. We were asked to step out so they could "roll" my dad. He was dead when we returned. 😭

Did I suspect foul play? Sure did. But 👺 When I tell you that our family was crippled in a moment, it's an understatement. I didn't know what to do. What to say. Where to go. I just knew that it would never be the same. I was alone again. I did not go home that night. I did not go home to Dana's either. I simply could not be around anyone. I'll turn my phone off and drive off. Cry. I'm a crier, people. It's my thing.

Bill was my biggest supporter. And now… he's gone.

When I moved to Hopatcong, Bill helped me with every problem I encountered. A relationship we did not have until 2017. I never felt like part of the family until then. I did not feel like Bill's "daughter" until I moved back. In fact, the Christmas prior, he asked me if I still wanted to be adopted. Something I always wanted but didn't want them to have to pay for.

He was the only person who understood what I was dealing with in regard to my mystery illness. He never made me feel like a burden. And now he's gone.

Now what will happen? Will I die alone? Will my family be ok?

The funeral was rough. I only remember bits and pieces. I spent the majority of the viewing time outside with my Uncle Jimmy. I just couldn't be in there. Uncle Jimmy was there with my Aunt Regina. Bill's sister. Aunt Regina was really sick during this time, and she was using a wheelchair. Jimmy was caring for her. My Aunt Regina was my Uncle Jimmy's whole world. 🤍 He was not taking her illness well. While we are outside, Jimmy will break down and pray that my Aunt Regina's sickness be transferred to him. 🙏 He could not deal with the fact that she might die. Said he would not be able to deal with it. Wanted to reverse the situation onto him. 😵

Jimmy was a great man. We hit it off on day one. He accepted me as his niece from the door. And his love for me showed through his actions and his words.

After the service, I'll return to my "normal" life of just waiting to die. I will start spending a lot of time at Dana's for the next month. I had promised Bill to make sure she was good before he had passed. I'm not sure how much longer I'll be around to help, and I didn't want any more regrets. I would have done this regardless of our agreement. And Bill knew that.

This transition was hard for me because me and Dana were truly never close. She was a wonderful parent to me, but we did not have much else. She was always so busy with my siblings that I never pushed the subject. I just tried to be an extra hand for her. I didn't want her to be alone. Because I couldn't deal with the thought of losing her too. 😣

This month, I will be placed on the medical marijuana program. I was not open to any of the pills that they were trying to shove down my throat. But the doctor was adamant about keeping my heart rate and blood pressure elevated and relieving some anxiety. My typical vital signs were critical at this point. 84/46 with my heart rate in the 40s and dipping into the 20s while I slept, but would peak to as high as 180 during an episode. All of my tests are returning normal, and they can't find a reason for the frequency of me passing out. POTS reacts differently in different people. This is when my cardiologist will start pushing the consideration of a pacemaker. 🤔 If my heart is okay, why would I need a pacemaker? No thanks. I'll figure this out on my own.

I just want to remind everyone that these are the moments that shaped my soul. This is not my life story. This is not to bad-mouth anyone or to portray anyone in a bad light. I harbor no animosity towards anyone, and I love and forgive every single person that has been mentioned or will be mentioned. And I probably will forever. 🙈 But I acknowledge everything for what it is.

End of November 2019. This one came with a lot of local rumors that deserve some clarity. I will meet someone who we will call Josh. Josh was a well-known business owner in town. We met accidentally. I was having some problems with my car, and he came highly recommended. Do you believe in love at first sight? Because this is truly what it was for me. The second our eyes met, I saw sparks.

These "sparks" will make me stupid.

Of course, we exchanged numbers before I left. He was "single." 🤥 He did everything right until he got me into his bed. Then all of a sudden, he was in a relationship? 🤨 Like I said, never been the jealous type. Hope it works out for you guys. And that's exactly the response that I gave him. 🙈 But it did not end there.

December, Dana tells me to go home. And stay there.

What did I do? 😔

Says I am smothering her. I was crushed. I was enjoying spending time with her. But I was also aware that she was dealing with her own grief at this time. So, I left and tried to stay away.

We are now in March 2020. Covid. World's falling apart. I'm still in the dark about what's happening to me medically. In my personal life, Josh would frequently reach out, supposedly over with his partner. I'm not one to verify the truth. And this man literally made me dumb. I absolutely could not control myself. And I definitely trust people more than I should. I continuously accept his lies. 🤚 And honestly, I suspected them. But again, in my head, I'm dying anyway. A moment of feeling wanted is better than nothing. This thought pattern will almost destroy me.

This BS has been going back and forth since November. What wasn't divulged about this situation was that Josh got me pregnant. Me, being the God lover that I am, took it as a sign. What can I say, people? I'm a hopeless romantic. I felt it was God telling me that he was the one and there was hope for my future. 🤡

When I confronted Josh about the baby, he did not take it well. He was angry. Made threats. Told me that if I didn't have an abortion, he would kill himself. 🙀 Looking back, I should have tried him on this. Please forgive me, Father, for my heartless words. 🙏

But my empathy for him, my saddened soul, my knowledge of what it would be like for my baby having a father that did not want them, pushed me to follow through with his wishes and I had it. It was not a smooth experience. There were complications. After this, I will get an IUD. I will never be in that position again.

I'd like to say that that's where it ended, but again, that would not be the truth.

We are now in June 2020. I'm still sick. Passing out but not as often. It's died down to a few times a week at this point. I've made some subtle changes to my diet; they seem to be helping. I'm not great, but I'm better than I was physically.

Mentally, I'm a mess. I still feel like I am in my last days. Single. Still avoiding Shane. Shane has threatened to take my children from me. His reasoning? Kids weren't safe with me passing out all the time.

I agree to let him stay in my basement for the girls. We are still not getting along. I will begin to spend as much time as possible out of my home. Mostly in my car. Driving around aimlessly. I simply could not be around him or in that house.

This is where I will have my "hoe" phase. Not really, but this is where I wasn't myself. I will not date. I will simply connect with people. Understand that I felt like this was all I had to offer anyone at this point. And I truly did not care. Not even a little. 🙈

If you "got" me during this time, you lucky as hell. 😂 Probably wouldn't have happened had it been a few months prior or a few months after.

I will add three bodies to my count this summer. 🙀 Such a hoe. 😂🙏 Only one decent guy in the bunch, and we didn't work out because of miscommunication. Although I was visiting with a purpose, I didn't want to feel like that was all I was. Just so happened that the last time I saw him, he was rushing to head out. I was honest with him about how he made me feel. 🙏 He was respectful and apologetic. But it was too late at that point.

Again, I was looking for someone to stand by my side while I died. Not run out on me. 🙀 What can I say? I was quite selfish at this point.

August 2020. I will once again reconnect with someone from my past. Do you see a pattern? Derek. He will introduce me to my new passion. Quadding. He truly showed up at a time my soul needed a purpose. 🙏 For the next three months, he will teach me how to ride safely on my dad's ATV. My dad always invited me out with him on it, but typically it was to hunt. I'm no killer. I am an aim-for-the-knees kind of woman. 😂 I just want you to stop pursuing me. What God decides you deserve is His choice.

Now I have a passion. 🤍 Every chance I get, I will try and convince Derek to take me out to the forest. I did not have a truck at this point. I had a small Elantra. I could not tow myself. Although I was learning how to every chance we went out.

September 13, 2020. Today I will pass out. This will be different from the usual incidents. I will have an "experience." I will be taken somewhere else. Mentally. I will see a desolate earth. Fires. I will have a conversation with a man about what will come.

I will return to consciousness. I will not be able to lift myself off the floor once I come to. Shane is there. My kids. Shane calls an ambulance. They load me up in the chair and take me to the emergency room.

Today I will be diagnosed with one final condition. CFS. Chronic fatigue syndrome. My "experience" will be disregarded and labeled as a lack of oxygen episode. I will be prescribed medication to help rebuild my muscles.

Once I return home, I will be thrown into a rabbit hole of spirituality. I needed answers for what I saw. Lack of oxygen wasn't cutting it for me.

Shane will trade in his Lancer for a Jeep and hand me the keys. His response? "Sorry for ruining your life." 🫠

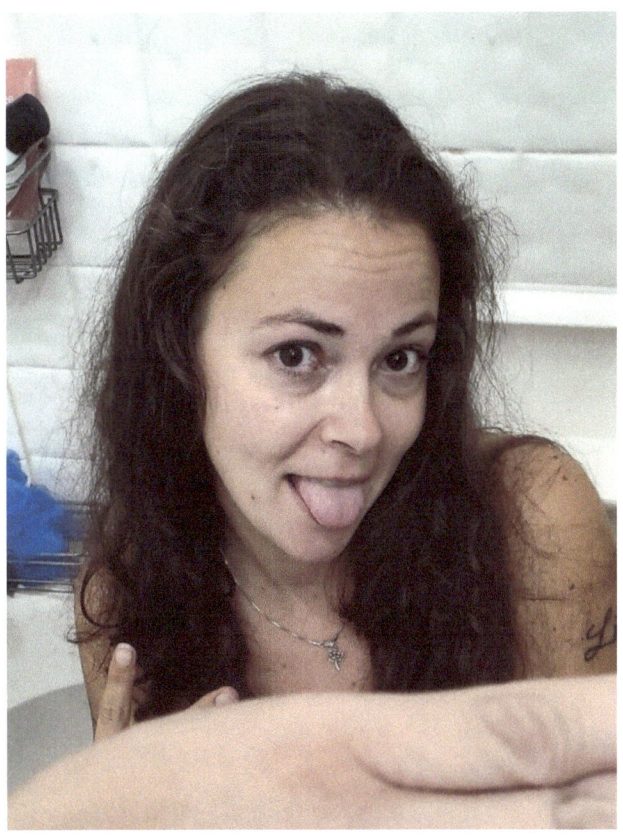

Released from the Hospital – 150 lbs of resilience. Still here. Still fighting.

Chapter 9
A Different Plan

Did I take those keys, you ask? I sure did. 🤷‍♀️🙏 I'm no dummy, people. This man wrecked my life. My kids' lives. Was a jeep going to fix that? Absolutely not. Was a jeep going to fix our relationship? Again… strong no. But this jeep will give me the freedom to pursue a newfound passion. By myself. Without having to depend on anyone else. So, I took it.

November 2020. This is where I will meet my next topic. We will call him Steve. Steve was Derek's friend. We met quadding. My intentions were not pure with him. He was hot… I was lonely… I instigated. In my eyes, Steve made sense. He was a mess emotionally, and so was I. He was just released from jail. Had been through some shit but overcame it. Did his time. Clearly unavailable emotionally. And neither of us were looking for a relationship. 🙈 Please remember… I'm waiting to die. We decided it best to keep it casual, and for the next few months, we will build a bond.

Me – Quadding ♡

January 2021. I have told Shane to leave. Again. Since September, I have only passed out twice. I'm over Shane threatening me with taking my girls. I tell him to file. He leaves. Again. And for good. He will take his jeep with him. March of 2021. Me and Steve will "officially" become a couple. I will take a loan out with Dana to purchase my own jeep. 🙏 Medically, Covid shots are being passed around like candy. I'm totally for protecting my mom. I head to my cardiologist appointment. The doctor spends quite some time explaining how the shot is affecting people with autoimmune conditions. He advises me against it. I don't argue. At this point, I'm deep down the rabbit hole of only needing God's help. And I'm vocal with everyone about it.

April 1st, 2021. Today I will lose my best friend Janelle. Janelle had agreed to get Avery from daycare for me. She wasn't feeling well. I will pick her up from Janelle's and bring her to the doctor. Avery will test PRESUMED positive for Covid. I will reach out to Janelle and let her know. Janelle will not take this well. Janelle's birthday was in a few days. She had plans to leave the state. This is when mandatory isolation was being required. She demands that I show her proof that Avery is really sick. I do not respond to her messages. Honestly, I was dumbfounded that her concern was not with my child. People were dying left and right. Obviously, we weren't trying to harm anyone. Janelle will show up to my house hostile. I will be calm. Ask her what she's doing there. Although Janelle only lived a few short blocks from me, she rarely came to my house. I always went to hers. She gets out of her car, comes up to my window, and starts screaming about how I am trying to ruin her plans. Hurt her family 😣 I would never. Says I don't care about her or her family. Then proceeds to tell me that I have 30 seconds to send proof or our friendship is over. It was already over at that point in my eyes. I tell her that as her best friend, she should just accept that what I was saying was the truth. I had never done anything to prove that I could not be trusted. She did not agree, continues to scream her point across. She finally leaves. I will send her proof, not to fix our friendship, but to satisfy her need of proving me a liar. I'm not. We will not speak for quite some time after this. She was dealing with her own issues at this time, I truly do not believe she wanted this outcome. But sometimes friendships grow apart, and the truth separates. 🙏

My entire house will be required to test. April 3, 2021. I have tested positive for Covid. Everyone else is good. Besides Avery, who is presumed positive but has no symptoms. I ask Shane to come stay with the kids so I can quarantine. He comes. During this time, Shane is not himself. He's undergoing his own mental issues where he now believes he is God. Not a God, but THEE God. 🙄 Not mine. 👻 In my eyes… he's the devil. Here to steal, kill, and destroy. Again, I've been on a spiritual dive since September, and I'm constantly studying. I've probably read most of the religious books available at this point. He's vocal about what he is experiencing, and people are concerned. I wasn't. I know fake when I see it, and Shane was trying to get a reaction. I will receive a call from DYFS at 2 am while I'm staying at the hotel outside of town trying to quarantine. DYFS tells me that I have 15 minutes to return home, or they were taking my girls. I arrive home. Super sick. I'm standing outside on my deck talking with DYFS about the situation. Explain that Shane is only there because I have been commanded to quarantine by the health department. He does not live in my house. They want Shane to go be evaluated at the hospital. He agrees and leaves via ambulance. They will keep him inpatient for the next week. This will cause chaos in my family. My girls did not take this situation well. Turns out DYFS was called by family that supposedly loved us. 🤪 You can keep your "made in China" love, and forget we exist. 👻 No hard feelings… just a no thanks. My kids deserve better than you. 🙏

End of April, I will return to the cardiologist for a follow-up. He will ask me if I received the Covid vaccine. 🤪 I'll explain to him that he advised me against it due to my condition. He will respond with "everyone should get it." I will ask him if there's new information or if anything changed. He will again give me the same response of "everyone should get it." My red flag detector is going off like crazy, and I sense he no longer has my best interest at heart. I truly felt like he couldn't care less if I lived or died. This will be the last time that I go to this cardiologist. I will spend the next few years searching for homeopathic remedies for my conditions.

June 2021, I will become a vegetarian. I will cut out all processed sugar and foods. These are main causes of body inflammation. I will start taking herbs and tinctures. Me and Steve are doing ok. Steve was the first "manly" man that I had dated. He liked to be outdoors. He liked to fix things. Stay busy. Steve had a child but did not have custody of her. She was a big part of why I wasn't in a rush for Steve living with me. I saw this little girl as myself, pleading for people to do her right. 🙏 She had already been through so much, I never wanted to be a negative in her life. I quickly grew to love this little girl as my own. Steve was well-behaved and well-mannered the first year we were together. He did not drink around me at all. He only smoked marijuana (to my knowledge). He really was trying to be better. He did everything right. Supported me, encouraged me, showed up when I needed someone. This is the first time in my life that I will experience the true meaning of a partner. Someone I could depend on.

July 2021, I will start working for a new company as an administrative assistant/sales processing. September 2021, I will receive my 2nd letter from DYFS that I am an ok parent. 😭 🙏 December 7th, 2021, I have confronted Steve about a message he publicly posted on Facebook about being a single dad a few weeks prior and for the girl to hit him up. 😵 I'm at a loss for words. See, I have done everything correctly this time. Differently. I have found my voice. When I approach things that trigger or bother me, I address them, something I have always struggled with doing. When people try and hit on me or show interest, I don't entertain. Steve has been staying at my house for almost a month at this point. Something I was hesitant about doing for many reasons, but mostly for his child. I really wanted his focus to be on her. And she had already sacrificed so much.

Steve has been drinking. When I try and get some clarification on what is going on, Steve will lose it. Starts raising his voice, getting angry. I sense this change and tell him I'm going to bring him home. Steve did not have a license. I did not feel safe. He loses it in the car. Starts punching things inside my truck... continuously. I pull over and ask him to get out. He refuses. I tell him we will just wait until someone comes. This makes him angrier. Starts grabbing for my keys. I try and block him. In this moment, I will catch an elbow to the face. He will then get out of my truck, throw my watch, and punch the outside of my passenger door, leaving a dent. I will drive home, leaving him a few blocks from my house.

Steve will call me the next morning, still intoxicated, screaming about coming to get his belongings. I tell him I will drop them off. He then makes threats that he's coming with his parents. 😨 Who I can hear in the background also making threats. Apple = tree. I do not feel safe. I do not want him anywhere near me or my children. I take his messages, voicemails, and evidence of his danger down to the police station. I file for a TRO. Due to my evidence and the marks I have on myself, I am granted one. Steve's father will come to pick up Steve's belongings with an officer. We will not speak again until the end of January when once again, I will be dumb. I will break the TRO and reach out to Steve. See, this side of Steve was not my Steve. This was a guy who popped up randomly, mostly when Steve decided to hang with his old pals. Steve's pals weren't his pals. They frequented the strip club where my cousin worked. They were known users. And I don't say that in a judgmental way. However, if you have a problem that you have overcome, you don't entertain the same crowd who has not. Nothing positive can come from that situation. They were trouble. They liked to see him low. See him struggling. That's the Steve they were used to. That's the Steve they wanted to stay. The fun Steve. Not me.

I had seen all of the progress that he had made. The things he had changed to be better. He fought to be a better partner, a better parent, a better person. And I couldn't unsee it. I missed him. And his daughter. I wanted us to make it work. Figure it out together. I knew I could help if I could get him to see that I truly was there for his best interest. Unlike his boys. I will testify on Steve's behalf. They will drop the TRO.

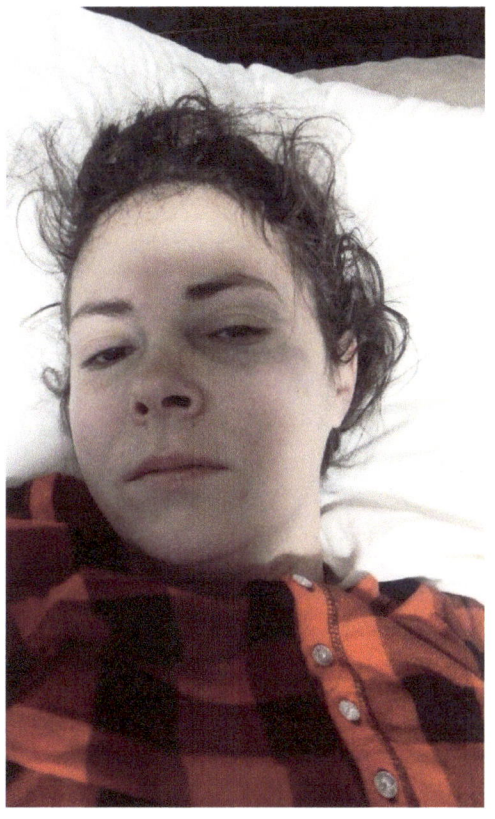

Result of Altercation with Steve – Taken After I Was Granted a TRO

February 2022, I will get to meet my nephew Nico and his family. ♡ They live in Delaware, about 4 hours away. I have spent a very long time searching for him and the rest of my biological family. Family has always been important to me because I never really had any. I have never belonged anywhere. I'm looking for people like me. I'm trying to understand why I am the way that I am. We will meet in the middle and spend the day at the aquarium in Camden. I haven't seen Nico since he was little. This is the first time I am meeting his family, his fiancée

Kaliah and their two kids. Kaliah has a heart like mine. So grateful for my nephew that he has this woman. ♡ We ended up getting a room for the night at the same hotel with adjoining rooms. Steve decides he wants to attend last minute, and I agree. Steve will once again drink. I'll be asleep. But he'll help intoxicate my nephew. NOT the first impression that I expected him to make. When I vocalize my concerns, he will tell me only Nico got drunk and not him. 😠 This will cause me to spend less time with him. Lessen my communication. I wanted him to get help. I wanted him to help himself.

End of April 2022, me and Steve will start speaking again. Here comes my toxic patterns. We will reattempt to make things work, but very slowly. We don't jump right back into dating. Just slowly start hanging out again. Quadding and smoking. Over the next two months, things will improve. Steve's no longer drinking. Really trying hard to stand by this decision. I was never much of a drinker, so this wasn't a big loss for me. Summer 2022, Steve will start casually drinking again with his pals. Two-beer limit. This will not last long. This summer we will go to High Point for the day with our girls. Once again, Steve will find a stranger to serve him beers. By the time we leave, he's drunk. Once again, screaming and yelling in my vehicle. I don't feel safe. I pull over on the road and take my daughter and keys from my vehicle. We walk down the block from my truck. We will be outside for roughly 15 minutes, leaving Steve and his daughter in my truck to cool down. Again… she is his. 😌 People do not understand that I cannot differentiate. Everyone gets the same love. Everyone. Steve is now outside my vehicle, screaming to leave. I will make a decision to go back to my truck for his daughter's sake. My only priority at this point is getting her back to his parents safely and going home. The next twenty minutes will be twenty minutes of hell. He will continuously make threats towards me. Towards my vehicle. He has zero nice things to say towards anyone. The more I tried to reason with him, the angrier he was. The girls are both hysterical in the back.

Steve calls them crybaby bitches. I tell him that he's ridiculous. He responds with, "I'll show you how ridiculous I am when I force this truck off the road." 💀 I will pull into a gas station and remove his belongings from my truck. Him and his child will get out. I will message Steve's dad and let him know I had to leave them in Newton. I will go home. Steve's dad will pick them up. The next day, Steve will message me as if nothing happened. He swore I was always lying. Even though there was always evidence and witnesses. He will tell me he loves me and will ask me to help him figure it out. Of course, I say yes. What can I say, people? I'm special. 🐖

Me and My Girls at Steve's Parents' Beach House

Due to my spiritual dive, (possibly a future book 📖 🙏) I no longer want to celebrate man-made holidays. 🎃 This year will be the first year I take the kids to the water park instead of celebrating Halloween. Steve's daughter will attend with us. This will turn into a vacation from hell. Please understand that at this point, Steve's patterns with attending any functions/parties ended in turmoil. This is what I most frequently try and do with my family—travel. Make memories. He had absolutely no self-control. But his daughter was with us, so I was feeling more confident. While spending the day at the water park, Steve has indulged in a few drinks. Please understand that Steve did what Steve wanted. There were no suggesting other options. That only escalated things quicker. It's nighttime. Steve's drunk. Steve's angry. He's cursing. Saying mean things. I try and calm him down. He just gets angrier. His daughter asks why he had to drink. Says that he ruins everything. (He truly did.) He turns his anger on his daughter... says she's a selfish bitch. 😡 Leaves the room. At this point, I reach out to Janelle. We have reconnected since our episode, and I need someone to be aware of what's going on. I let her know I fucked up. And we are now stuck in the hotel with a very intoxicated man who is making us all feel unsafe. Part of me wants to get a separate room, but I cannot because of Steve's daughter. She is his. Not mine. 😔 I finally get the girls to fall asleep before Steve returns to the room.

The next morning, we will leave first thing. Steve remembers nothing. This was a common response after sobering up, pretending not to remember. This moment will be the beginning of the end. This should have been the final straw for me... but I could not abandon that little girl. She needed her dad. He desperately needed help. If I didn't help ... Who would? I mean, at this point I think everyone can tell how many friends Steve truly had. And the 🌴 that's been bailing him out his whole life. Even though we won't officially end for almost another year, the next 6 months me and Steve will frequently separate. He just can't stop drinking and we were all tired of him promising to be better. Especially my daughter Adriana. And she's vocal to Steve about his shortcomings. Quite the opposite of me. With very little empathy for the bullshit.

May 2023, Steve has agreed to seek outside help. He has agreed that him and alcohol are not a good match. We are finally making progress on the real reasons he is trying to drown himself. I'm hopeful. He's really focusing on work and his child. These were the moments for me. 🙏 When he showed up as his best self. Very hard to do when you are driven by ego and pride. This will continue for the next two months. In my family life, June 3rd, 2023, my nephew and his fiancée have had their final baby. 🤍 Lydia. She was born absolutely perfect. At this point in our relationship, I am closer with his fiancée than I am with him. Kaliah was a pure spirit. Like I said before, I'm so grateful that my nephew has this angel. 🙏 We instantly connected since the moment we met. She was an absolute blessing to everyone. Really made me regret not living closer to them. We could absolutely be the best of friends. 🙏 Love you so much, girl. Thank you for loving me and my children 🤍 I was sad I couldn't watch their children grow up. That we weren't closer as a family 😔 But as we all know… my life has been quite hectic since moving back to Hopatcong. They will open their doors a few days later for my daughter and she will arrive as her regular unhelpful teenage self. They will have to send her home earlier than expected. This broke my heart. I really wanted her to be me in this moment. Helpful. But I forgot to allow her to be herself. Which was a typical teenager. A very intense learning moment for me as a parent. Definitely caused a rift between me and Adriana for a few weeks. Until I acknowledged that my disappointment was my projection, and I apologized to her. Love you always baby. 🤍🙏

Out of nowhere, Steve will once again get the urge to see his old pals. I was not a fan. These pals only brought destruction, and I was vocal about that. I questioned him on it, and he swears his intentions are pure and he's going to bring his daughter with him to make sure he doesn't drink. I tell him it's a bad idea. He tells me to trust him. Swears everything will be fine. He leaves. We all have plans for the next day to go to the Land of Make Believe. We were all excited. Steve will not come home. Steve will get drunk… leave the house with his child at ten pm… alone and drunk… walking the main road of Rockaway after ten pm. Steve will be jumped. In front of his daughter. Steve will have his teeth knocked out. He will be arrested. His daughter will be released to Steve's parents. Steve's dad will reach out the next morning and let me know what has happened. Tells me Steve loves me and will call me as soon as he can. 🙁 I was absolutely heartbroken for what he had put his daughter through. I loved this man. Truly. I only wanted the best for him and his daughter. I told him that nothing good would come from that choice and he chose to ignore my warning. If he could put his own child's safety at risk, why would I assume my children would be different? I could not unsee this situation. I had many emotions running through me for the next few days.

Steve is finally released. He has seen the light and now wants to make me his wife. 🥴 He can't be around his daughter, so he gets a room in Rockaway. I visit him, but not romantically. I need to know why shit happened the way it did. I get no answers. Just false promises that shit will be different. I decide to take a step back and not "date" him anymore. From August to September, we were not official but trying to figure out how and if we wanted to move forward.

September 2023, I will be invited quadding with my neighbors. These were close neighbors of mine. I frequently hung around them. They were good people. I felt safe with them. A feeling that's always been hard to come by for me 🧎 I wanted to go. Steve was not invited due to his own previously displayed behaviors. The neighbors were not a fan of his issues and honestly, I didn't blame them. He didn't want me to go, but I was never one to not do what I wanted. I truly ask for nothing. 👏 NOTHING 👏 I have always had my own things. And I have always paid my own bills. Even during the times we were together, he basically

114

paid for his gas from me bringing him to and from work, weed, and food. 👺 I've never needed anyone's money. I like having my own things so they can't be taken away. And I spent 15 years with someone who threw every "gift" in my face. So, I went. I had an amazing time. Met some great people. I will barely speak to Steve while I'm gone. My cell service was really bad. Although I did speak to him a few times, it wasn't enough in his eyes. I will be called a slut and a liar. Along with a whole bunch of other choice words. Remember… we are not together. I'm deciding whether I still want this. And this was the moment that decided for me. After everything this man showed me… put me through… my kids… his kid… I'm a slut? Because I went quadding with my neighbors? What? I will be very vocal with Steve about never wanting a relationship with him again. Definitely not with someone who thought so lowly of me. If that's what I am... then so be it. But I'll be that alone. 👋 I wish you guys the best. 🙏 Be safe. And that was that. I'm not begging anyone ever again to treat me like a person. You want someone who fills those cracks… go find them. Especially when I was always true, open, and honest. 👆 Is not love.

The First Photo I Took After Leaving Steve

115

Steve will jump into a new relationship a few weeks later. His new supply was the opposite of me. And she will reach out in December to let me know that he has her now. ♡ 🧎 No one can make me jealous over someone I tried my absolute hardest with. He deserved this woman… not me. They will get married a few months later due to a baby 👶 This is when me and my neighbor will become best friends. So grateful for you, Sara. 🧎 ♡ Love you always. October 2023. I will go on my first official date. This guy was very different from the men I normally date. He was funny, empathetic, could hold a conversation, was educated, had manners, no criminal history, no hidden kids, safe… marriage material. We hit it off pretty quickly. I was honestly turned on by his confidence. It's hard to come by these days. We had a great time. We will see each other two more times before this fades. Bad timing, I suppose, but 👶.

November will be my final self-destructive decision. We will call this one Ron. Now… going in, I had pure intentions. Ron was nice. Friendly. He was related to someone else who is in my story. I needed some work done and he was suggested to me. Once I arrive, we take a ride to take care of some errands. We stop at the liquor store so he can grab some drinks. Asks if I want anything. I'm not a drinker. There are many reasons why I chose to drink this time. 🥴 I am not perfect people, and I am trying to drown my feelings. I will get some tequila. Once we get back, he invites me out for a drive. We make our drinks and head out. That's the last clear decision I remember making. Choices were made this night that are not remembered clearly. I had more to drink than I had anticipated and stayed the night. 🤯 When I woke up the next morning and realized what had happened, I was overwhelmed with emotions. I knew I fucked up. For the next week, I will try and correct my wrong. My efforts go unnoticed until I stop trying. Once I acknowledge that I ruined this connection, we will no longer communicate. This is the only man who can call me a slut. My behaviors were just that. Unacceptable and honestly disgusting. I won't drink again after this.

End of December 2023. Here comes my past once again. Israel has reemerged. Very apologetic for our previous experience. I was sympathetic due to our childhood, while still very aware that he had already presented himself. This man was wrecked. He liked toxic women. He liked chaos. Thrived in it. He could not make any decisions for himself. He allowed his mother to run his life. Desperately wanted me to be in a relationship with him. All my Spidey senses said no. There were a lot of things going on at the time that told me he could not be trusted. And the more vocal I was about him having secrets, the more secrets were exposed. Since my experience, I know things that I shouldn't. Secrets. Betrayals. Absolutely horrible things. But I don't say much. I'm waiting for everything to come to the light. God's timing.

This December I will be told that it makes more sense for me to get my name changed instead of being adopted. 🫶 I will wait to take my future husband's last name only. It was the principle for me. This was the absolute moment that I realized who I was to everyone since my dad had passed. Again, these are my feelings. The moments that shaped my soul. And no one owes me anything. My dad loved me. If I'm nothing, then that's what I will be. Anything anyone needed in my family, I was always quick to run and help. Decisions that caused a lot of problems within my relationships. I was constantly being told that I would run to my mom's for her every need, putting everyone else behind. 😔 Again, this is what I do. Help.

January 10th, 2024. I get a phone call from the police. Adriana is at the station, and I need to come down. I leave work and head to Hopatcong. Get to the station. Adriana has been attacked. She has been sexually assaulted by a 19-year-old man. She is a mess. The cops were unsympathetic, with the exception of one officer. Basically, saying it was her fault. 😡 This is my 15-year-old baby. I don't care what you believe. If she says he raped her... he raped her. I take her down to the hospital to get a kit started. We file charges. We go home.

For the next two months, I will search for services myself. All available resources given to us were for adults. Like usual, there is no one to help. If nothing else, New Jersey is consistent. Just a constant disappointment. We are still receiving in-home therapy support from Caring Partners, but our therapist hasn't been seen in weeks. When my daughter needs services the most. Adriana is a wreck. She barely sleeps. When she's able to sleep and is awoken, she will wake in terror. Defensive. She will no longer allow anyone to touch her. She will be placed on at-home instruction. She no longer felt safe being around boys. Around anyone. She barely leaves her bed. 🏠 I will finally find a place to help Adriana. Ginnie's House. We will have to screen for services. Adriana will be approved for no-cost therapy through this facility. 🙏 We will attend weekly appointments.

End of February 2024, my mother will dismiss the money I borrowed from her the previous year. A little over $3,000. Typically, I would borrow throughout the year and repay her once I got my taxes. 🙏 We truly needed this money.

March 10th, 2024, I will go to get my hair highlighted with my sister Mary. I miss our old relationship, and I want to try and fix it. I head to Pennsylvania. We have an amazing time. Grab some dinner afterwards at a Mexican restaurant across from the salon. I order vegetarian as usual. A margarita. Food was okay, however, the second I finish my meal, I am sick. 🏠 I mean I am sick. I cannot stop throwing up. I am now driving my sister home, about twenty-five minutes from the salon. In the snow... using an extra-large coffee cup to collect my throw-up. I will spend this entire drive continuously apologizing to my sister for me being sick. I get her home and head to go get my girls from Pop's house about an hour away. It's around 7 pm. Roads are absolutely horrible, and I get detoured and end up lost for about an extra hour. I finally make it to Pop's. I have been throwing up for about 3 hours at this point, and I make a decision to stay instead of driving home. I'm in absolutely no shape to drive. I will spend the night curled up in a ball on the recliner, almost filling a paint bucket with throw-up and praying for God to heal me. I make it through the night… I have not slept at all. I climb myself into the tub, my go-to place since I originally got sick. Say one final prayer for healing and pass out from sleep deprivation. I will awake to cold water and will feel completely healed. 🙏 I'll take my girls and head home.

From March to May, Israel will do the absolute most to destroy my peace while portraying himself as a god to my children. Basically, giving them whatever they wanted regardless of my wishes. He will place trackers on my vehicle. Three separate times that I will find myself. He will record me without my consent. He will break into my accounts. Social media… emails… bank… my phone carrier… you name it. He will recruit my child to help betray me. He will kick my bedroom door in. The more I tried to be understanding and compassionate, the less I wanted him around. He was always doing the absolute most while pretending to be the absolute best. He swore I was the one up to no good. 😤 Bro… I am exactly who I say I am. I literally do nothing. Work, come home, sleep, rinse… repeat… recycle. Enjoy your search. I was tired. I was not trying to convince him to stay around. The only thing he was doing for me was stressing me out. If anything, I was being compassionate about his mental issues but still keeping my distance.

May 2, 2024. Once again DYFS will arrive at my home. Kristen. This woman was different. She was compassionate and understanding of our family situation and what we were experiencing since January. Says that the call didn't have much warrant regardless. Says that she will recommend closing out our case. I am still waiting for my third letter to let me know that I am an okay parent. 😅

May 24, 2024. Israel has lost his shit once again. A few hours prior he was supposed to attend hockey practice, he attended his ex instead. At her home. Lied about it to me. 🤬 Whatever, I'm nothing. And he was a liar. I knew this. What he didn't know was that I had said a prayer to remove him from my life if he meant us no good. Literally three hours prior to this. 🙏 My faith is unbreakable, people. He decides he wants to go through my phone again. 🙄 I'm asleep. My daughter has allowed him in. They are quite close at this point. He has brainwashed my daughter into believing that him continuously breaking the law was for my benefit. ☠️

I have not disclosed the information I found a few hours earlier to her. I am not one to involve my children in grown people's problems, especially after what my daughter has already been through. I need her to feel safe. This man was not safe. Not for anyone. He's now trying to wake me. It's after midnight. I finally wake up and ask what's up. He says, "I need to get into your phone; can you put the password in? Because it's not working." I say no, roll back over, and try to fall asleep. He gets angry and tries to argue with me. I tell him I changed it because he's a liar and has no business going through my things. A boundary he was never okay with. He says he's going to break it. I just respond with, "Do whatever you got to do. I'm going to bed." The phone is not important to me. I really couldn't have cared less. He takes my new phone and spends the night in his truck trying to break in. He's unsuccessful. I wake up at six, go to get my phone from him. He's hostile. He hasn't slept. At this point, I'm over him and his bullshit. I want my phone, and I want him to leave me the fu*k alone. I take my phone. He has put it on some lock, and I'm angry. I tell him to remove it. He says no. I tell him to leave. He says no, says he wants his stuff. He has his foot blocking my door. I tell him to move his foot, and I'll bring it down. He responds with, "I'll move my foot once you bring my stuff down." I run upstairs. While I'm upstairs, I hear him and Adriana arguing. He pushes my door. Adriana is there. She starts screaming at him to leave. I run back downstairs to see what's going on. Adriana is now screaming at the top of her lungs. I'm trying to push the door shut. I'm now panicking about the situation. I start screaming. This is not me. I don't respond like this. But I did. All I care about at this point is my children's safety. I tell Adriana to call the police. She does. He leaves.

May 28th, Israel will show up at my job. He will try to run me off the road in his jeep. He will then follow me to a local park. He will come up to my passenger window and ask me to talk. I will tell him that there is nothing to talk about. Arguing with this man never went anywhere. Ever. Just endless rambling. And I am absolutely over it at this point. My doors are locked, and my window is cracked. He will get angry, punch my passenger side window, and almost break it. He will then reach inside my window, unlock my door, and climb in. I once again tell him that I do not want to talk, that I do not feel safe, and that I want him to leave me alone. He responds with, "I don't care what you want." We are alone. I am visibly shaking with fear. He continues to ramble for about 30 minutes before I am able to convince him out of my jeep. I will return to work and message his mother about what happened. She will tell me that she is going to have him evaluated and will make sure he leaves me alone. She begs me not to involve the police. Israel has about 3 months left on parole, and she doesn't want him in any more trouble. I am vocal with her about me and my children's safety and how it should be top priority at this point. When his mother confronts him about this situation, he will lie and say he never came to my job. 😵 Liars gonna lie. Whatever, dude… leave me the hell alone. I don't want to get anyone in trouble ever. But when it comes to safety, I'll do whatever I have to like always.

May 29th. I will wake to two flat tires on my truck, three flat tires on my quad. It has been less than 24 hours since his mother said she would handle it. Sure seems to be handled. I will have to borrow money from Dana to fix my truck and the quad. I had just returned to work May 20th. I needed to take emergency family leave due to the situation Adriana had experienced. Adriana is still actively struggling with everyday life, and suicide is a constant in her mind. We were all affected. We all needed therapy. We had very little money during this time. We were frequently visiting food pantries just for everyday needs. My "emergency" family leave won't be approved until 12 weeks after returning to work.

As for Adriana's court case… her attacker is claiming mental illness. They want her attacker to be evaluated. This has been going on for months. My daughter was one of many of this man's victims, and he was currently facing another charge in a different county. This was the prosecutor's way of justifying the delays. Clearly, we were not going to receive any vindication from these people. They weren't sympathetic or compassionate about Adriana. She was but a mere number at this point. They gave more time and compassion to her attacker. Prosecutor Caroline Murray was more worried about her retirement than my child's life. My family's life 😭 Sick fu*ken world.

June 3rd. My week-old cameras have been disconnected for the night. My house has been broken into. My jeep keys are missing. I call the police. The police have been frequent flyers to my home the past 6 months. They show up… I tell them everything. I mean EVERYTHING. About the tracker. NJ A3591. I show photographic evidence. About the account hacking. N.J.S.A. 2C: 20-25. Again, showing photographic evidence. About his harassment. N.J.S.A. 2C:33-4. Again, providing proof. About my tires being slashed. A total of 5 top-end tires. Two cooper with Kevlar on my truck. About $300 a piece and 3 on my quad. Just under a grand. Way over misdemeanor value. They will take my report. I'll have to borrow money from Dana to have my truck rekeyed. Please remember that me and my children are barely getting by currently. Tonight, me and my kids will stay by Dana's. I didn't feel safe. 12 am, I will get a call from the police about suspicious activity at my house. I will return to meet them. They will once again take fingerprints. In this moment, I will realize that a silver necklace with my dad's picture inside is missing. They will ask for specifics, which I provide. They will leave, and I'll return to Dana's for the night. The next five days will be quiet.

June 8th, 2024. Sara is helping me set up some cameras that I had to purchase. As we are doing the install, Sara sees a drone flying above us. In this moment, I run into my basement. I had grabbed my dad's drone two weeks prior from my mother's. I wanted to take it out quadding with me. Guess what's missing? I tell Sara it's my dad's drone and that Israel has it. We hop in my jeep and drive down the block to where we saw it head. As we get to the corner… here comes Israel doing 100mph. I pull out after him. He dips off a side street. Lost. It's a dead end. Cars on both sides. I position my truck slightly sideways so I'm hard to get around. I get out and wait for him to turn around. In this moment, Sara is in my truck calling the police, who have frequented my home so often at this point that they ask if she is Sara from Knox. 🤭 🙏 Sure is. She tells them what's going on and where we are. Israel has stopped his vehicle because I am blocking the road. I ask him for my dad's drone. He tells me it's his, but he has my dad's at his house. 😵 He needs to leave and is vocal. Says he's on an ankle monitor and needs to be home in 6 minutes. Why are you flying drones above my house? He says he needs to talk to me. No thanks. Cops finally arrive. I explain what happened. They are well aware of what I have been dealing with. They allow him to leave and tell him he has to return my dad's drone. There is still an open investigation about what's been going on, but understand that I am fully aware that this town clearly does not care about me or my family. Or our safety.

June 10th, I will meet his mother at the police station in town. We will exchange belongings. I will be very vocal about my expectations for Israel to stay away from me and my family. She says she will try. I respond with, "If she cannot… I will involve God on my behalf." She does not take this response well. She believed in God heavily, but her spirit and actions proved that we were not praying to the same one. 🙏 For those of you who know… you know. 🐵

July 19, 2024. This will be the last time I speak with Josh. He has arrived at my home expecting me to fall for his bs like usual. This time will be different. I am not interested in him continuing this toxic pattern. I deny access. He leaves. 👋

August 2024, my children and I will go on my first family vacation with Dana and all of my siblings. We are finally going to spread my dad's ashes. This vacation is something I never experienced. My siblings are my REAL siblings in my head. Like I said… Everyone gets the same love from me. Always. I always envisioned us having an unbreakable bond, sharing secrets, and being there when it mattered most. The relationship I experienced my cousins having during my time with my Aunt Judy. But I never had this. 😔 Maybe a little with my sister Mary, about two years when I first left Shane. But other than that, I had more of a connection to Bill's older daughters, who lived far away. Peg and Sam. They always welcomed me as their sibling and treated/talked to me well. We just never saw each other. 🙏 Love you guys. I think my younger siblings always saw me as the help. I mean this in the most humble way. They really only saw me when my parents would ask me to come over and clean or for holidays. I was always paid for my services, and it became a little inside joke that they referred to me as Consuela. But this hurt me. Although I never spoke on my feelings. Again, I learned very early to take every blow as a blessing. I just always laughed it off and dismissed it. Nonetheless, me and my children will have an amazing time on this vacation. Other than me getting a serious bone infection that will require emergency surgery once I return.

September 2024, I will have emergency surgery on my jaw. They will have to pull my molar. I will spend 4 days in the hospital. Sara will accompany me until I'm admitted. She will be the only person to see me. I will get no other visitors at all. Mid-September, I will get a call from the police that they didn't find anything regarding what Israel had put us through. And they are closing the investigation. 😣 This town is a joke. Everyone is corrupt.

End of September, I will be told that my family is withholding the fact that I'm part of the family. 😣 Specifics don't matter, but it involved my brother. They said that legally I am nothing and that it was no one's business. 🥺 I have never been in trouble. I have never been someone to be ashamed of. And being told to change my name instead of being adopted was still very present on my heart. This was the second moment that crushed my soul. I would have given my last breath for every single person in my family, and I am nothing? I felt like I was being torn down intentionally. Where is my dad? I have always shown up to be nothing other than a blessing. If Bill never arrived in Lodi and invited me back in 2008, I would have never come back. I was content with the fact I wasn't part of their family and that they owed me nothing 💔 Once again… Thank you. It feels great. I will take a step back from offering any extra help to ANYONE at this point. This was the last time I was going to allow anyone to make me feel like this. If I am nothing? Call someone else.

October 11, 2024. Adriana's court case. Sentencing for her attacker has finally arrived. 9 months later. He is given 3 years. 😔 3 years with time served. I know people who got more time being caught with marijuana. 🥺 This man will qualify for parole at 16 months, and he will once again be released into the public. 💔 He already had 7 reports against him. Ephesians 6:12 "For our struggle is not against flesh and blood, but against the rulers, against the authorities, against the powers of this dark world and against the spiritual forces of evil in the heavenly realms." Prosecutor Murray, our judge, our support, was a joke. I cannot say that I expected anything different after the lack of justice I received from the police. All I see are patterns of injustice. Where the attacker wins. Do you know what it's like to not feel safe in your home? In your vehicle? In the world? We had NO ONE fighting on our behalf. My family had Sara, James (a very close neighbor), and Bernadette (James's wife). These were the only people checking to make sure we were safe. People fail to realize that my faith lays in the most high God. Not man. And ALL the books will tell you that this…. Is Satan's world. 🐯

October – December, my housing and my income will be targeted. 😔 I will surrender all control to God and retreat back into my focus on him. 🙏 Since then… Our lives have been ok. James 4:7 submit yourselves unto God. Resist the devil and he will flee from you. ♡ 🙏

Chapter 10
39 Years of Building Character

So here we are, at the lessons. I have learned that no matter how much you love someone… No matter how long you invest… If it is not for you, it will never be for you. I wanted to take people with me who were content with being alone, never changing, never growing. People who allowed others to tell them who they were. At any point, someone can choose better. Soften their heart. Admit defeat and sit with their flaws. But most don't. I have learned that you cannot force anyone to take a different path. Even if the path you present is the better choice. Love will always be the answer. Compassion. Forgiveness. Patience. But never tolerance. What you don't address will continue to present. Do the work. Don't you ever drop yourself below someone else. We are all one diagnosis/accident away from a completely different life. I now know that the longer you spend chasing the mistakes from the past, the longer you prolong your arrival to your present. There's a reason the windshield is larger than the rearview. And sometimes people are only there for a season. Like leaves on a tree. Let them fall away. Real ones can't be lost. I have learned that people only listen to their ability to respond. Not to comprehend. If they heard one side of the story and believed it, that's how they feel about you. 🙇 Don't try and change their minds. People want you to explain to them why you don't want to be around them. Why you cut them off. I'm not about to tell a grown person what they did wrong. 🤚 You know what you did. Stand on it. Take it with your chest out like I did.

I have learned that most people will have your back when you are at your highest but abandon you in your lowest. You must show up for yourself. You must decide who you are and never change for anyone. And most importantly, that I cannot change anyone's heart. I should believe it the second it's presented. A mask can only stay on for so long. And evil loves to be displayed. Am I perfect? Absolutely not. But I don't REQUIRE perfection. People grow when they feel safe, heard, respected. A perfect life is built, not found. And without a solid foundation… it will never stand. We as people are that foundation. I am 39 years old. I have been with 12 people sexually in my life. (My 12 demons) 🫣🙏 Definitely cannot refer to any as disciples. None were sent from GOD. These are decisions I chose. The paths I thought I wanted at the time. Living in lust. In my sin. Forgetting who I truly am. I have sat in the darkness since forever. I am attracted to it. It seems to be where I feel most at home. The abuse I endured molded my heart into accepting it as normal. I was trained for this abuse. It took me my whole life to realize why I continuously chose the same path. And it was the simplest explanation. I have never chosen myself. Not once. I always chose what benefits everyone else. I have been protecting my inner child by invalidating myself as a person. As a priority. It was never a lack of self-love. Like I said, I have always loved myself. But I've always known that no matter what I endured, I would be okay. God got me. And I truly felt like others needed love more than me.

Since as long as I can remember, I have had the same prayer on my heart. And that was for God to place me in the lives of those who needed me the most. 🙏❤️ Always. I have always known that I was different. That my faith was different. The more I tried to fit in, the more I couldn't help but stand out. I'm not cocky or conceited. I am confident in who God called me to be. Psalms 139: 10-18: "Even there your hand will guide me, Your right hand will hold me fast. If I say, "Surely the darkness will hide me and the light become night around me," even the darkness will not be dark to you; The night will shine like the day, For darkness is as light to you. For you created my inmost being; You knit me together in my mother's womb. I praise you because I am fearfully and wonderfully made; Your works are wonderful, I know that full well. My frame was not hidden from you when I was made in the secret place, when I was woven together in the depths of the earth. Your eyes saw my unformed body; All the days ordained for me were written in your book Before one of them came to be. How precious to me are your thoughts, God! How vast is the sum of them! Were I to count them, they would outnumber the grains of sand—When I awake, I am still with you." I have never thought that I was better than anyone else. In fact, I spent the majority of my life feeling sorry for existing. As if I were a burden. As if there was something wrong with me because I cared. I am not perfect. I continuously chose the wrong path. But my God is faithful. Thessalonians 3:3 "The Lord will strengthen me and protect me from the evil one." He makes no mistakes. Although I fall short of his glory, I remind myself of Corinthians 10:13. "No temptation has overtaken you that is not common to man. God is faithful, and he will not let you be tempted beyond your ability, but with the temptation he will also provide the way of escape, that you may be able to endure it." I have been called to test the spirit. 1 John 4:1. "Beloved, do not believe every spirit, but test the spirits to see whether they are from God, for many false prophets have gone out into the world." And Ephesians 2:8 "For by grace you have been saved through faith. And this is not your own doing; it is the gift of God." He has always been faithful. He has always shown up on my behalf. Exodus 14:14 "The Lord will fight for me. I only need to be still."

I was chasing safety from people who were certain to put me in danger. People who had proven to me time after time that I meant nothing. I already had everything I needed. Within myself. After everything I have endured, I am so grateful and thankful that it never changed my heart. That I am still able to love unconditionally. That I am able to be optimistic. That I still feel joy by helping others. 🙏 Especially those who don't deserve it. Who am I to make the decision of who is worthy? I am no one. I don't regret anything that I have overcome. Every bump in my road molded my heart into exactly who God wanted me to be. Into whom he has called me to be. Song of Solomon 6:3 "I am my beloved's, and he is mine. He browses among the lilies." I am not afraid anymore. I keep Matthew 8:26 in my heart. "Why are you fearful, o thee of little faith?" People who have hurt me think they have won. What you have won is a chance at a harder path. This heart I have is not my own. My spirit cannot be crushed. My light will never be dimmed. Leviticus 6:12-13, which states, "And the fire on the altar shall be kept burning on it; it shall not be put out. And the priest shall burn wood on it every morning and lay the burnt offering in order on it; and he shall burn on it the fat of the peace offerings. A fire shall always be burning on the altar; it shall never go out." Ever. Psalms 91:1 "He who dwells in the shelter of the Most High will abide in the shadow of the Almighty."

Me and My Children

I am the gift. My heart is the gift that God has sent to the darkness in this world. Every single person who has crossed my path was predetermined before my birth. Nothing is by chance. These people needed me the most and the love I have to offer. My brush with death changed me. My personal experience forced my eyes open. My faith will never waiver. I know that I do not deserve God's grace, but He has been faithful to me nonetheless. I am fully aware that my light illuminates people's darkness, but He has created me to sit with people in that darkness. 🙏 Show people another way. I don't see addicts or abusers. I see people. Hurt people. We are all traumatized and broken. But we can help each other. We can all win together. At any point, we can all decide that we want better and change. I know that God has big plans for me. I know that everything that has happened to me has been for me. 🙏 I will never fail. Romans 8:31 "If God is for me, who can be against me?" People cannot destroy me because I own all of my mistakes. And if I could go back in time and choose differently, I would not. I was made for this. My mistakes do not define me. My character does, and even that isn't set in stone. For a definition does not leave room for growth. And I am always growing. My heart and my fruit will outweigh any lie told behind my back. John 3:20-21 "Everyone who does evil hates the light and will not come into the light for fear that their deeds will be exposed. But whoever lives by the truth comes into the light, so that it may be seen plainly that what they have done has been done in the sight of God."

People lie when they are scared. You have to realize that NOTHING in this world truly belongs to you. And that at any moment, it can all be taken away. Once you accept this, you can never be controlled again. 🙏 Everything is for God's glory. People assume that because I don't speak about things, that I don't know things. Or that I am slow. Naïve. Easy to get over on. I promise you that it is the exact opposite. I know a lot more than I let on. I'm giving you the opportunity to show me who you are. Like I said, people talk. I want to know who you are for myself. If I addressed everything that I know, I wouldn't have a story. I would not have had friends. I wasn't sent to condemn anyone. I might encourage you to change your behavior, but I can't do the work for anyone. Sometimes it takes 39 years to realize that you're standing in your own way. Change is hard. Scary.

It's been the people closest to me that have always betrayed me the most. People who say they love me while praying for my downfall. 🙏 People who say they love me and then do the exact opposite of love. People who secretly envy me and carry jealousy in their hearts. Snakes. The only reason I believe in love is because of how "I" love. I cannot be the only person on this planet with a heart like mine. The love I have for others has never been a weakness. It has been a light. A candle in the darkness. The reason I am able to get up every morning and face the day with grace. And humility. And even after everything, I still love you. And I'm going to continue to pray for your heart to change. Until a person feels safe, they will never address the reasons why they self-sabotage. Trauma is everywhere.

Instead of giving my light away to people who do not appreciate it, I've been keeping it to myself. I no longer want to save anyone. I no longer seek abuse. Toxicity. I don't need years for you to show me who you are. I saw it. I believe you. Be safe. I'm not better than anyone… I'm just not one to compare. Like I said before, you're not me, and I have no interest in being you. I love me. That's enough now. No… I don't want to get drunk and make bad decisions. No, I don't want to come over and tell you what I have going on in my life so you can gossip about me once I leave. I'll pass on pretending to be friends with people who want to tear me or anyone else down. No, I don't want to sit in your face and pretend to not know what you have done to me or said about me. There's been ample time for changed behavior. Remorse. It's a strong no for those who had all access to me but abused their power. I run from those who've shown me who they are. Be that person. Over there. It's never from a hurtful place. Just a no thanks. Everyone gets exactly what they deserve according to God's glory. I have learned to release what was never mine to carry 🐱 if it is not sent directly from God, I'm going to pass. I am safe in God's hands; I need but to stay still, and I have learned to love my solitude. So, no…it doesn't hurt. Not anymore. Rejection is God's protection.

Me and Avery – May 2025, Five Months into Freedom

I have learned that there is absolutely nothing wrong with lifting people up. Being that extra hand. A shoulder. An ear. Your voice may be the voice that saves someone. If we all helped each other instead of judging one another and tearing each other down, maybe this world could be different. Instead of viewing people as a lost cause, maybe offer some assistance. Some time. Sit with them. Talk with them. Try and understand. I'm going to continue to offer my time, my service, and my love to people who need it. I'm going to continue to be that surprise voice of encouragement. I will always show up as my best self. I will continue to wear my heart on my sleeve. Always. We change the world by healing one heart at a time. But don't ever let it be at your expense. Sometimes you have to show people you love them by letting them lose you. It may have taken me 100+ times to accept that someone wasn't for me, but once I believe it, there's no turning back. I still love you... but you can no longer have the same me. Now I got to show up as you. Now I must treat you the same way that you treated me. And no, there's not much remorse. Because I naturally have a soft heart. If I have to switch it up, it's because that's the only way you will truly comprehend that I am serious. If you wanted me to speak better about you, then you should have been better. And if you don't take time to acknowledge what you have, don't be upset when God takes it away. 🐵

I have learned that people want you to miss them. So, you chase them. People forget that you can't miss what you have never had. If you never showed up for me... loved me... respected me... helped me... What am I missing? The abuse? The disrespect? The lack of compassion and accountability? But those who have harmed me... You're going to feel my loss. You're going to miss my unconditional love and forgiveness. 🙏 My grace. How you could always depend on me being there regardless of the situation. How I was ready to rock with you at your lowest. I may not mean much to the people I love, but I have always known how important I was to God. That's enough. I know I was sent here on a mission. I have always been vocal about how He shows up on my behalf. Literally my whole life. The majority of my abusers, claimed to be godly people. Which God? 🤭 My God will show you exactly who I am. People think I'm playing until their lives fall apart. Psalms 105:15 "Touch not my anointed and do my prophets no harm." Because no one else loved me, God loved me. Although I am not religious, I'm ok with being called the crazy bible lady. Like I said, I have never fit in. God has always shown up for me. God has always rescued me. He has fought all of my battles. God has been faithful to me in my most disgusting moments. If you can't see that within my entire story, then you haven't been paying attention. I have always been surrounded by angels. I'm chasing that love. The love that has been proven to be true. Yeah… I go through it. But I am carried through it. 🙏

How much would you sell your soul for? I cannot expect to live a life any easier than what others have endured. John 15:18-27: "If the world hates you, keep in mind that it hated me first. If you belonged to the world, it would love you as its own. As it is, you do not belong to the world, but I have chosen you out of the world. That is why the world hates you. Remember what I told you: 'A servant is not greater than his master.' If they persecuted me, they will persecute you also. If they obeyed my teaching, they will obey yours also. They will treat you this way because of my name, for they do not know the one who sent me. If I had not come and spoken to them, they would not be guilty of sin; but now they have no excuse for their sin. Whoever hates me hates my Father as well. If I had not done among them the works no one else did, they would not be guilty of sin. As it is, they have seen, and yet they have hated both me and my Father. But this is to fulfill what is written in their Law: 'They hated me without reason.' "When the Advocate comes, whom I will send to you from the Father—the Spirit of truth who goes out from the Father—he will testify about me. And you also must testify, for you have been with me from the beginning." And Colossians 3:12: "Put on therefore, as the elect of God, holy and beloved, bowels of mercies, kindness, humbleness of mind, meekness, longsuffering." What keeps me different is the pursuit. I'm not chasing the things others are chasing. I don't care for material things or status. I'm content with enough. I don't want to be the hottest female in the room. Or the baddest b*tch. I want to be safe. I want to love and be loved correctly. I want to help people. I want to show up as exactly who I have been called to be. Like always. I haven't changed because I have never been anyone other than myself. If you want to know how I am treating someone else, it's the same way that I have treated you. I do this in real life y'all. 😇 I want to show everyone the power of faith. Romans 13:4

"For he is God's servant for your good. But if you do wrong, be afraid, for he does not bear the sword in vain. For he is the servant of God, an avenger who carries out God's wrath on the wrongdoer." No matter what happens, I will overcome. For Isaiah 54:17 states, "No weapon formed against you shall prosper, and every tongue which rises against you in judgment you shall condemn. This is the heritage of the servants of the Lord, and their righteousness is from Me," says the Lord. So no, I will no longer pretend to be ok with injustice. I'm going to call it like I see it. And remove myself for myself.

People ask me why I continuously show up for those who harm me, and my answer is simple. I'm going to always be me, what you choose to do with me, is between you and God. God sees all. And He knows my heart. I needed to make the mistakes I have made, to realize they weren't for me. It's none of my business what others think of me. And honestly, I couldn't care less. Gossip comes from people who can't have you or people who can't compete. But I promise you that loose lips… sink ships. And tea is nice, but it stains. If they are talking to you, they are most definitely talking about you. A true leader will never be found in a crowd. What you allow will most definitely continue. If you stand for nothing, you will fall for everything. If you aren't going to fight for you… who will? And my most favorite Psalms 16:8 "I keep my eyes always on the most high. With Him at my right hand, I will not be shaken." People should focus on their own sins… because God's not going to ask you about mine. He's been updated. 😅 I will continue to rise every morning and carry my cross. Until the day my justice is delivered and presented before the public. The day my vindication arrives from the evil that has conspired in the darkness. Then and only then, will I sit down and shut up. But until then, I suppose maybe I can get started on book #2? 😅 🙏 We are living in dark times people. And evil is absolutely everywhere. Stay focused my friends. And endure until the end.

www.ingramcontent.com/pod-product-compliance
Lightning Source LLC
Chambersburg PA
CBHW040845120626
46547CB00001B/30